Emperor of Hindustan Jahangir

Wakiat-i Jahangiri

Emperor of Hindustan Jahangir

Wakiat-i Jahangiri

ISBN/EAN: 9783337113537

Printed in Europe, USA, Canada, Australia, Japan

Cover: Foto ©Andreas Hilbeck / pixelio.de

More available books at **www.hansebooks.com**

WAKI'ĀT-I JAHĀNGIRI.

First Edition :   Calcutta 1875

First Pakistani Reprint :   Lahore 1975

Serial No. of Publication   809

Edition :   500

Reproduced by :

SHEIKH MUBARAK ALI.

Publishers & Booksellers.

Inside Lohari Gate, Lahore (Pakistan)

Telephone No :   64327

Price in Pakistan :   Rs. 20.00

Export Price :   U.S. $ 2.50

HAFIAZ PRESS.LHE.

PREFACE

Henry Miers Elliot was son of the Late John Elliot Esq., of Pinlico Lodge, Westminister. He was born in the year 1808 and was educated at Winchester and entered the Venerable College of William of Wykeham at the age of ten years. During his stay there, he devoted himself to the institutions and shared in its distinctions having gained both the silver medals for speaking. When he left Winchester, his proficiency in the Oriental Languages proved so remarkable that the examiners at the India House placed him alone in an honourary class. He had thus good fortune to arrive in Calcutta with a reputation that his future career tended not only to maintain but to exalt. After performing distinguished services at different places in India, he died at the early age of 45 while seeking to restore his broken health in the equable climate of the Cape of Good Hope.

In 1846, Sir H. M. Elliot printed the first volume of his "Supplement to the Glossary of Indian Terms." The Glossary itself was a pretentious work then meditated and for which great preparations had been made by the various local governments.

In 1849, Sir H. M. Elliot publishsd the first volume of his "Bibliographical Index to the Historians of Muhammadan India".

The history of the reign of Jahangir depends almost entirely on the memoirs written by himself or under his directions. It has long been known that there were different works claiming to be autobiographies of Jahangir. Wakiat-i-Jahangiri was an important attempt which Sir H. M. Elliot undertook with the help of some other famous writers. He gathered the selected informations from the original memoirs (Tuzk-i-Jahangiri) and compiled them in a very concised form giving the whole picture of the reign of Jahangir.

Lahore.   Publishers

January, 1975

LIST OF CONTENTS

Chapter		Pages
1st year of the reign	...	15
2nd ,, ,, ,, ,,	...	27
3rd ,. ,, ,, ,,	...	41
4th ,, ,, ,, ,,	..	45
5th ,, ,, ,, ,,	...	46
6th ,, ,, ,, ,,	...	49
7th ., ,, ,, ,,	...	51
8th ,, ,, ,, ,,	...	59
9th ., ., ,, ,,	...	63
10th .. .. ., ,,	...	66
11th ,, ,,	..	71
12th ., ,, .,	...	76
13th . .. ,.	...	81
14th ., ., ,, ,,	...	91
15th ,. ., ., ,,	...	98
16th ., ,. ,, ,,		103
17th ,, ., ,, .,		108
18th ,. ,.	...	111
19th ., ., ,,	..	115
20th ..		121

WÁKI'ÁT-I JAHÁNGIRI.

WE now proceed to consider the authentic Memoirs of Jahángír. At the outset we are met with a difficulty about the proper name to ascribe to this autobiography, and the matter has been slightly alluded to in the preceding article. The names which are given to the Memoirs, whether spurious or genuine, vary greatly. Besides the *Tárikh-i Salím-Sháhí* and *Túzak-i Jahángiri*, they are also called *Kár-náma Jahángiri*,[1] the *Wáki'át-i Jahángiri*, the *Bayáz-i Jahángir*, the *Ikbál-náma*, the *Jahángir-náma*,[2] and the *Makálát-i Jahángiri*.[3]

Muhammad Háshim, in the Preface to his *Muntakhabu-l Lubáb*, quotes among his authorities three several *Jahángir-námas*: first, that by Jahángír himself; second, that by Mu'tamad Khán; third, that by Mirzá Kámgár, entitled *Ghairat Khán*, which was composed in order to correct sundry errors into which Mu'tamad Khán had fallen. Neither of these works is specially entitled to the name, the first being the "Memoirs," the second the *Ikbál-náma*[4] *Jahángiri*, and the third the *Ma-ásir-i Jahángiri*.

[1] *Critical Essays on Various Manuscript Works*, p. 40. It is the name given to Ardisbír's account of his travels and enterprises which was circulated by Naushírwán for the improvement of his subjects.—Malcolm's *History of Persia*, vol. i. p. 95.

[2] *Ma-ásiru-l Umará*, Preface. *Crit. Essay*, p. 39. Preface to *Tárikh-i Shahádat*, by Muhammad Bakhsh Ashob. Preface to the *Akhbár-i Muhabbat*. Preface to 4to. vol. of *Tárikh-i Nádiru-z Zamání*.

[3] *Mir-át-i Aftáb-numá*, MS., p. 382.

[4] This word, signifying "a record of prosperity," is a common term applicable to panegyrical history. It is adopted in India in imitation of the great poet Nizámí, the second part of his *Sikandar-náma* being so entitled.

I prefer calling this work the *Wáki'át-i Jahángírí*, as being not only in conformity with the title usually given to the auto-biography of Bábar, but as being the one ascribed to it by the author of the *Mir-át-i A'ftáb-numá*, and as being in a measure authorized by a passage in the Memoirs themselves under the transactions of the first year of the reign. *Jahángír-náma* and *Bayáz* would also appear to be not unauthorized by different passages of the Memoirs. Perhaps *Malfuzát*, after the precedent of Tímúr's Memoirs, might have been more appropriate; but no author has ever quoted them under that designation.

Gladwin, who extracts from the work in the "Reign of Jahángír," published in A.D. 1788, speaks of them under the name of *Túzak-i Jahángiri*, which he says are the Commentaries of the Emperor written by himself. In the catalogue of Captain Jonathan Scott's Library the *Túzak* is said to be the same as the *Ma-ásir-i Jahángiri*, which is altogether wrong.

The copy of the authentic work which I have had an opportunity of examining is in the possession of Major-General T. P. Smith, of the Bengal Army. It was copied for him at Lucknow, and at his desire collated by Saiyid Muhammad Khán, who procured with much trouble copies for the purpose of comparison from the Libraries of the King of Dehlí, Rájá Raghúband Singh, chief of U'chhaira, Nawáb Faiz 'Alí Khán of Jhajjar, and several other places, and completed his task in the year 1843. A copy was sent to England for deposit in the Library of the East India House.

This work is prefaced by an Introduction and Conclusion by Muhammad Hádí, which will be noticed in another article. The autobiography is almost entirely different from the one translated by Major Price, and it may, therefore, perhaps be considered worthy of being translated, if it were only for the purpose of displacing the spurious version already given to the world, and which has attracted much observation from its supposed authenticity.

It is written in the form of Annals, giving chronologically

tho occurrences of each year of the reign. Major Price's translation, on tho contrary, gives very few dates. The stylo is
simple and inornate, and bears in some places the marks of
negligence.

The royal author speaks of two different copies of his own
Memoirs, tho first edition comprising tho period of twelve years
only. In the transactions of the thirteenth year of the reign he
tells us, that when the occurrences (*wakái'*) of twelve years were
transcribed from the *Jahángir-náma* into a fair copy (*bayáz*[1]), he
directed the writers of the Royal Library to make several copies
of the history of these twelve years, and to bind them into a
separate volume, and then he distributed them amongst his dependents for circulation throughout his dominions, in order that
they might become a study and exemplar for their observance.
The first copy which was prepared he presented to Sháh Jahán,
after writing on the back of it with his own hand the date and
place of presentation. A little later, in the annals of the same
year, we read of two more copies being given away.

The twelve-year work ends with the King's arrival at
Ahmadábád in Gujarát, which occurred at the beginning of
the thirteenth year of the reign. In the language there is no
difference between that and the complete Memoirs, and in the
former there are very few omissions, not amounting to more than
500 lines, so that it is evident that it was not re-compiled for the
purpose of being included in the complete work. I have seen
two copies, both commencing and ending in the same way; but,
from several omissions, one was a third less than the other. The
best contained 482 pages of 13 lines each.

This smaller work is evidently the one which Gladwin speaks
of in his " Memoirs of Jahángír." He says (p. 92), " They con-
tain a minute account of the political and private conduct of his
life from the commencement of his reign to the end of the
twelfth year. They are universally admired for the purity,
elegance, and simplicity of the style, and he appears in general

---

[1] Usually a common-place book. The word also means "paper," "whiteness."

to have exposed his own follies and weaknesses with great candour and fidelity. When he had completed the Memoirs of twelve years, he distributed several copies of them amongst his children and the principal officers of his Court. He continued these Memoirs with his own hand till the commencement of the seventeenth year of his reign, when, finding himself from ill-health unable to proceed, he from that period to the time of his death employed Mu'tamad Khán as his amanuensis. The whole of the continuation is exceedingly scarce; the compiler of this history not having been able to procure a sight of any other copy than the one which was lent him by his friend Colonel Polier."

It will be observed hereafter that the name of the continuator is wrongly given, and that the real Memoir is extant to the end of the eighteenth, or rather the beginning of the nineteenth year.

That Gladwin never saw the larger work is probable from the style in which he speaks of the Memoirs above, and from his extracting nothing from them after the twelfth year, as well as from the tables of routes at the end of the history, which do not extend beyond Jahángír's arrival at Mándú, which occurred in the twelfth year of the reign, leaving out all the subsequent pro-gresses to and from Gujarát, and in Upper India and Kashmír. It is doubtful whether Colonel Polier's copy, to which he alludes, contained the continuation ascribed to Mu'tamad Khán, or the continuation by the Emperor himself beyond the first twelve years, or merely the Memoirs of these twelve years.

It is strange that the author of the *Ma-ásiru-l Umará*, who was a man of unusually large research, quotes in his Preface the *Jahángír-náma*, written by the Emperor, "in which he details the occurrences of twelve years of the reign," so that he, too, could not have been in possession of a perfect copy, and we may therefore consider the Memoirs of eighteen years as a very rare work, almost unknown even in India itself. The author of the *Critical Essay* is among the few to whom it was known, because he says he never saw a copy which extended beyond the eighteenth year.

Respecting this more perfect work, Jahángír himself says in the annals of the seventeenth year of his reign, "On the 7th of the month of A'zur, the ambassadors of Sháh 'Abbás, who had been deputed several times to my Court, received honorary dresses, and took their leave. Sháh 'Abbás had despatched by Haidar Beg a letter to me, apologizing for his conduct in the matter of Kandahár. An account of it with the attendant circumstances was entered in this *Ikbál-náma*. * * *

" As I still suffered from the weakness which had affected me during the last two years, I had neither heart nor head to think about the foul copies of my Memoirs. It was about this time that Mu'tamad Khán returned from the Dakhin and kissed the threshold. He was a faithful servant and pupil, and conducted himself to my satisfaction. He knew my disposition, and understood me in every respect. He was before this employed to write the occurrences (*wakái*) of my reign, and I now gave him an order to continue the Memoirs from the date up to which I had been writing, and place his narrative at the end of my foul copies (*musawidát*). I told him to write it in the form of a diary (*roznámcha*), and after submitting it for my corrections, it was afterwards to be copied into a book (*bayáz*). Moreover, at this time my mind was seriously engaged in making preparations for the expedition to Kandahár, and distracted by the anxiety I sustained upon learning the disaffection and excesses of Khurram."

It does not appear that Mu'tamad Khán ever strictly carried into effect the wishes of his royal master; and it is probable he never did anything more than abridge his master's original, and after adding the concluding events, he compiled, under his own name, the work called *Ikbál-náma*, which will shortly come under review.

Jahángír seems to have rewritten the events subsequent to the twelfth year about the same period that he left off adding to his Journal, for he sometimes alludes to events subsequent to that of the date of which he gives the occurrences. In the account, for instance, of the celestial phenomenon, which he records in the thirteenth year, he says the effects of it were felt for eight years subsequently.

Before concluding this notice, it may be as well to observe, that the probable reason for the rarity of this volume is to be found in the fact that, in the latter parts of it, the conduct of Sháh Jahán towards his father is so severely reproved that it would not have been safe to copy the work, that it was consequently suppressed through fear of Sháh Jahán, and that after his long reign, it became almost forgotten, till the time of Muhammad Sháh, when fortunately Muhammad Hádí undertook to edit it.

This will appear more probable, if we consider the following passage, which occurs in the seventeenth year of the reign, on the occasion of Jahángír's march towards Thatta, to oppose his rebellious son. " I directed that henceforward he should be called ' Wretch,' and whenever the word ' Wretch ' occurs in this *Ikbál-náma*, it is he who is intended. I can safely assert that the kindness and instruction which I have bestowed upon him no King has ever yet bestowed upon a son. The favours which my respected father showed to my brothers I have shown ever to his servants. I exalted his titles, made him lord of a standard and drum, as may be seen recorded in this *Ikbál-náma*, and the fact cannot be concealed from the readers of it. The pen cannot describe all that I have done for him, nor can I recount my own grief, or mention the anguish and weakness which oppress me in this hot climate, which is so injurious to my health, especially during these journeys and marchings which I am obliged to make in pursuit of him who is no longer my son. Many nobles, too, who have been long disciplined under me, and would now have been available against the Uzbeks and the Kazilbáshes, have, through his perfidy, met with their due punishment. May God in His mercy enable me to bear up against all these calamities ! What is most grievous for me to bear is this, that this is the very time when my sons and nobles should have emulated each other in recovering Kandahár and Khurásán, the loss of which so deeply affects the honour of this empire, and to effect which this 'Wretch' is the only obstacle, so that the invasion of Kandahár is indefinitely postponed. I trust in God that I may shortly be relieved of this anxiety!"

No one could well have ventured to give currency to such imprecations during the life of Sháh Jahán. The same objection would not apply to the twelve-year Memoirs, because in them he is mentioned throughout in extravagant terms of laudation.

[The present autobiography is longer than the one translated by Major Price. It is a plain and apparently ingenuous record of all that its author deemed worthy of note. The volume contains a good deal of matter quite uninteresting to a European reader, such as the promotions and honours bestowed upon the Emperor's followers, and the presents he gave and received; but taken as a whole, the work is very interesting, and assuming that Jahángír is mainly responsible for its authorship, it proves him to have been a man of no common ability. He records his weaknesses, and confesses his faults, with candour, and a perusal of this work alone would leave a favourable impression both of his character and talents. Like his father, he was fond of jewels, and estimated their value as a true connoisseur. He was a mighty hunter, and took pleasure in sport, even in the later years of his life. He was a lover of nature, both animate and inanimate, and viewed it with a shrewd and observant eye. He mentions the peculiarities of many animals and birds, and shows that he watched their habits with diligence and perseverance. Trees and fruits and flowers also come under his observation, and he gives his opinions upon architecture and gardening like one who had bestowed time and thought upon them. The Extracts which follow will enable the reader to form his opinion of the work. They have been translated by various hands, some by Sir H. M. Elliot, much by his private *munshi*, some by a person whose handwriting is unknown to the Editor, some by the Editor, and from the beginning of the fifteenth year entirely by the Editor himself. The MS. translation of several years appears to be nearly perfect, but only a small portion of it can be printed in this volume.]

SIZE.—Small folio, containing 659 pages, of 15 lines to a page. [The copy belonging to the Royal Asiatic Society is also a small folio of 823 pages, of 15 lines each.]

The commencement of both works is the same :—

از عنایات بیغایات الهی یکساعت نجومی از روز پنجشنبه هشتم جمادی الثانی هزار و چهارده هجری گذشت در دار الخلافت آگره در عمر سی و هشت سالگی بر تخت سلطنت جلوس نمودم

The *Dwázda-Sála Jahángírí* concludes at about the 150th line of the thirteenth year of the perfect Memoirs; but as the same sentence is continued in them, it is probable that the real conclusion is, as one of my copies represents a few lines above, where he indulges in his complaint of the climate of Gujarát, and especially of Ahmadábád, which he said should be called Gardábád, the City of Dust ; Samúmábád, the City of Pestilential Winds, and Jahannamábád, the City of Hell.

هم درین وقت خانعالم که نزد دارائئ ایران بایلچئ گری رفت بود بگذشت باز آشنائ که بزبان فارسی اکبر می گویند پیشکش فرستاده بود از نظر گذشت

The conclusion of the larger work is as follows :—

دست تعرض از دامان ناموس و خانمانان او کوتاه است بفراغ خاطر روانه گردد و اگر توقف را مصلحت خود میداند هرگو که ازین ملک التماس نماید میفرمائیم

The copy in the King of Dehlí's Library gives the answer of Ibráhím Khán as part of the autobiography. In General Smith's copy it forms part of the continuation by Muhammad Hádí.

EXTRACTS.

[On Thursday, the 8th Jumada-s sani, 1014 Hijra (12th October, 1605), I ascended the throne at Agra, in the thirty-eighth year of my age.]

The Chain of Justice.

[The first order which I issued was for the setting up of a Chain of Justice, so that if the officers of the Courts of Justice should fail in the investigation of the complaints of the oppressed, and in granting them redress, the injured persons might come to this chain and shake it, and so give notice of their wrongs. I ordered that the chain should be made of pure gold, and be thirty *gaz* long, with sixty bells upon it. The weight of it was four Hindústání *mans*, equal to thirty-two *mans* of 'Irák. One end was firmly attached to a battlement of the fort of Ágra, the other to a stone column on the bank of the river.][1]

The Twelve Institutes.

[I established twelve ordinances to be observed, and to be the common rule of practice throughout my dominions.

1. *Prohibition of cesses (zakát).*—I forbad the levy of duties under the names of *tamghá* and *mir-bahrí*,[2] together with the taxes of all descriptions which the *jágírdárs* of every *súba* and *sarkár* had been in the habit of exacting for their own benefit.

2. *Regulation about highway robbery and theft.*—In those roads which were the scenes of robbery and theft, and in those portions of road which were far from habitations, the *jágírdárs* of the neighbourhood were to build a *saráí* or a mosque, and they were to sink a well, to be the means of promoting cultivation, and to induce people to settle there. If these places were

---

[1] See note, *suprá*, p. 262.

[2] [Price has "*sermohary*" instead of *mir-bahrí;* but although his MS. is indistinct, there can be no doubt that *mir-bahrí* is the term used. His MS. reads "*zakát, mir-bahrí,* and *tamghá.*" But in all the MSS. of this version, "*zakát*" is part of the rubric. The words "three sources of revenue" which Price uses are not found in his text.]

near to *khálisa* lands, the Government officials were to carry out these provisions.

3. *Free inheritance of property of deceased persons.*—Firstly. No one was to open the packages of merchants on the roads without their consent. Secondly. When any infidel or Musulman died in any part of my dominions, his property and effects were to be allowed to descend by inheritance, without interference from any one. When there was no heir, then officers were to be appointed to take charge of the property, and to expend it according to the law of Islám, in building mosques and *saráis*, in repairing broken bridges, and in digging tanks and wells.

4. *Of wine and all kinds of intoxicating liquors.*—Wine,[1] and every sort of intoxicating liquor is forbidden, and must neither be made nor sold; although I myself have been accustomed to take wine, and from my eighteenth year to the present, which is the thirty-eighth year of my age, have regularly partaken of it. In early days, when I craved for drink, I sometimes took as many as twenty cups of double-distilled liquor. In course of time it took great effect upon me, and I set about reducing the quantity. In the period of seven years I brought it down to five or six cups. My times of drinking varied. Sometimes I began when two or three hours of the day remained, sometimes I took it at night and a little in the day. So it was until my thirtieth year, when I resolved to drink only at night, and at present I drink it only to promote digestion of my food.

5. *Prohibition of the taking possession of houses, and of cutting off the noses and ears of criminals.*—No one was to take up his abode in the dwelling of another. I made an order prohibiting every one from cutting off the noses or ears of criminals for any offence, and I made a vow to heaven that I would never inflict this punishment on any one.

6. *Prohibition of Ghasbi.*[2]—The officers of the *khálisa* lands and the *jágírdárs* are not to take the lands of the *ráiyats* by

---

[1] *Sharáb*, lit. drink. Commonly used to signify wine, but spirits are included.

[2] In law, taking the property of another without his consent.

force, and cultivate them on their own account. The collectors of the ˙khálisa lands and the *jágirdárs* are not without permission to form connexions with the people in their districts.

7. *Building of hospitals and appointment of physicians to attend the sick.*—Hospitals were to be built in large cities, and doctors were to be appointed to attend the sick. The expenses were to be paid from the royal treasury.

8. *Prohibition of the slaughter of animals on certain days.*— In imitation of my honoured father, I directed that every year from the 18th of Rabí'u-l awwal, my birthday, no animals should be slaughtered for a number of days corresponding to the years of my age. In every week, also, two days were to be exempted from slaughter : Thursday, the day of my accession, and Sunday, the birthday of my father.

9. *Respect paid to the Sunday.*—He (my father) used to hold Sunday blessed, and to pay it great respect, because it is dedicated to the Great Luminary, and because it is the day on which the Creation was begun. Throughout my dominions this was to be one of the days on which killing animals is interdicted.

10. *General confirmation of mansabs and jágirs.*—I issued a general order that the *mansabs* and *jágirs* of my father's servants should be confirmed, and afterwards I increased the old *mansabs* according to the merit of each individual. He who held ten was not advanced to less than twelve, and the augmentation was sometimes as much as from ten to thirty or forty. The allowance ('alúfa) of all the *ahadis* was advanced from ten to fifteen, and the monthly pay of all the domestics (*shágird-pesha*) was from ten to twelve or ten to twenty. The attendants upon the female apartments of my father were advanced according to their position and connexions from ten to twelve, or ten to twenty.

11. *Confirmation of aima lands.*—The *aima* and *madad-ma'ásh* lands throughout my dominions, which are devoted to the purposes of prayer and praise, I confirmed according to the terms of the grant in the hands of each grantee. Mírán, *Sadr-i Jahán,* who is of the purest race of Saiyids in Hindústán, and

held the office of *Sadr* in the days of my father, was directed to look after the poor every day.

12. *Amnesty for all prisoners in forts and in prisons of every kind.*—All prisoners who had been long confined in forts or shut up in prisons, I ordered to be set free.]

New names for the Coins.

[Gold and silver coins of various weights were struck, to each one of which 'I gave a distinct name. The coin of 100 *tolas* I called *Nŭr-i sháhí;* the 50 *tolas, Nŭr-i sultáni;* the 20 *tolas, Nŭr-i daulat;* the 10 *tolas, Nŭr-i karm;* the 5 *tolas, Nŭr-i mihr;* the 1 *tola, Nŭr-i jaháni;* the ½ *tola, Nŭráni;* the ¼ *tola, Rawáji.* Silver coins.—I called the 100 *tolas, Kaukab-i táli';* the 50 *tolas, Kaukab-i bakht;* the 5 *tolas, Kaukab-i sa'd;* the 1 *tola, Jahángíri;* the ½ *tola, Sultáni;* the ¼ *tola, Aishyári;* the 10th of a *tola, Khair-kabŭl.* The copper coins in like manner each received a name.] [*Legends on the coins.*]

Hardás Ráí, who had received from my father the title of Ráí Ráyán, and from me that of Rájá Bikramájít (after one of the most celebrated Rájás of Hindústán, the founder of an Indian Observatory), was honoured by me with marks of the highest distinction. I made him commandant of artillery, with directions to keep 50,000 gunners and 3000 gun-carriages always in a state of readiness. Bikramájít was a Khatrí by caste. He was in my father's time examiner of the expenditure on the elephants, and was afterwards raised to the exalted grade of *diwán,* and enrolled among the nobles of the Court. He was not destitute of gallantry and judgment.

As it was my intention to satisfy, as far as possible, all the old dependents of my father, I issued orders to the *bakhshis,* that every one of them who wished to obtain a *jágir* in his own country must apply for a grant to that effect, and that, in accordance with the Institutes of Changíz, he should be rewarded with an *Altamghá* grant, and enjoy the same without apprehension of change or removal. My ancestors, whenever they wished to bestow a *jágir* in proprietary right, used to stamp the grant with an *Altamghá* seal, which means one to which red ink is applied. I ordered that the place of the seal should be covered with gold-leaf, and then stamped with the *Altamghá* seal. Hence I named it *Altúntamghá*—that is, the gold seal.

Mirzá Sultán, the favourite son of Mirzá Sháh Rukh, and grandson of Mirzá Sulaimán, the descendant of Mirzá Sultán Abú Sa'íd, chief of Badakhshán, was elevated to the grade of 1000. I had asked my father to allow him to be on my establishment. Hence I brought him up, and treated him as a son. Bháo Singh, the ablest son of Rájá Mán Singh, was rewarded by a *mansab* of 1500, retaining his former office, and Zamáná Beg, son of Ghayúr Beg Kábulí, had gained the dignity of 500, by serving me when I was Prince as an Ahadí. He now, having received the title of Mahábat Khán and a *mansab* of 1500, was nominated paymaster of my household. Rájá Nar Singh Deo, one of the Bundela Rájpúts, stood high in my favour. He was as brave, kind-hearted, and pure as any man of his age. I elevated him to the dignity of 3000. The cause of his elevation was the murder of Abú-l Fazl, a descendant of one of the Shaikhs of Hindústán, distinguished for his talents and wisdom. About the close of my father's reign, Abú-l Fazl, wearing upon his plausible exterior the jewel of probity, which he sold to my father at high price, was summoned from his appointment in the Dakhin to the Royal Court. He was not my friend. He inwardly nourished evil intentions towards me, and did not scruple to speak ill of me.

Murder of Abú-l Fazl.

The details of the murder of Shaikh Abú-l Fazl are thus described : Certain vagabonds had caused a misunderstanding between me and my father. / The bearing of the Shaikh fully convinced me that if he were allowed to arrive at Court, he would do everything in his power to augment the indignation of my father against me, and ultimately prevent my ever appearing before him. Under this apprehension, I negociated with Nar Singh Deo. His country lay on the high road of the Shaikh from the Dakhin, and he at that period was engaged on a plundering expedition. I sent him a message, inviting him to annihilate Shaikh Abú-l Fazl on his journey, with promises of favours and considerable rewards. Nar Singh Deo agreed to this, and God rendered his aid to the success of the enterprise. When the Shaikh passed through his territory, the Rájá closed upon him and his followers. They were in a short time put to flight, and he himself murdered. His head was sent to me at Allahábád. Although my father was exasperated at this catastrophe, yet in the end I was able to visit him without any anxiety or apprehension, and by degrees his sorrow wore away, and he received me with friendliness.

Discussion with learned Hindús.

One day I observed to some learned Hindús that if the foundation of their religion rested upon their belief in the ten incarnate gods, it was entirely absurd; because in this case it became necessary to admit that the Almighty, who is infinite, must be endowed with a definite breadth, length, and depth. If they meant that in these bodies the supreme light was visible, it is equally visible in all things, it is not limited to them alone; and that if they said that these incarnate gods were the emblems of His particular attributes, it is also not admissible, for, amongst the people of all religions, there have flourished persons who performed miracles, and were possessed of much greater power and talents than others of their time. After a long discourse, they at last admitted that there was a God who had no corporeal form, and of whom they had no definite notion. They said that as to understand that singular and invisible Being was beyond their comprehension, they could not form any idea of Him but by the means of some natural objects, and therefore they had made these ten figures the medium of raising their minds up to

the Supreme God. I then told them that they could not attain
that end by this means.

Portrait of the Emperor Akbar.

My father used to hold discourse with learned men of all
persuasions, particularly with the Pandits and the intelligent
persons of Hindústán.   Though he was illiterate,[1] yet from constantly conversing with learned and clever persons, his language
was so polished, that no one could discover from his conversation
that he was entirely uneducated.   He understood even the
elegancies of poetry and prose so well, that it is impossible to
conceive any one more proficient.   The following is a description
of his person.   He was of middling stature, but with a tendency
to be tall, wheat-colour complexion, rather inclining to dark than
fair, black eyes and eyebrows, stout body, open forehead and
chest, long arms and hands.   There was a fleshy wart, about the
size of a small pea, on the left side of his nose, which appeared
exceedingly beautiful, and which was considered very auspicious
by physiognomists, who said that it was the sign of immense
riches and increasing prosperity.   He had a very loud voice,
and a very elegant and pleasant way of speech.   His manners
and habits were quite different from those of other persons, and
his visage was full of godly dignity.

First Year of the Reign.[2]

Remission of Transit Duties.

As I had removed the practice of levying transit duties, which
amounted to many *krors* of rupees, throughout all the protected
territories, I also extended the same indulgence to all the
commercial places on the way between Kábul and Hindústán,

---

[1] [The word used is ﺍﻣﻰ "one who can neither read nor write, an idiot."]

[2] [Jahángír counts the years of his reign by the solar reckoning, and the first year
of his reign as commencing on the New Year's Day next after his accession, with the
entrance of the Sun into Aries, which corresponded with th. 11th Zi-l ka'da, 1014
A.H. (10th March, 1606 A.D.).].

the transit duties of which were collected annually to the amount of one *kror* and twenty-three *lacs* of *dáms*. The whole transit duties of both provinces, viz. Kábul and Kandahár, were paid to the public treasury, and they formed the principal part of the income of those provinces. I removed the practice altogether, and this contributed much to the prosperity and benefit of the people of Írán and Túrán.

Flight and Rebellion of Prince Khusrú.[1]

[In the first year after my accession Khusrú, influenced by the petulance and pride which accompany youth, by his want of experience and prudence, and by the encouragement of evil companions, got some absurd notions into his head. In the time of my father's illness some short-sighted men, trembling for their crimes and despairing of pardon, conceived the idea of raising him to the throne, and of placing the reins of the State in his hands. They never reflected that sovereignty and government cannot be managed and regulated by men of limited intelligence. The Supreme Dispenser of Justice gives this high mission to those whom he chooses, and it is not every one that can becomingly wear the robes of royalty.

The vain dreams of Khusrú and his foolish companions could end in nothing but trouble and disgrace; so when I obtained the sovereignty, I confined (*girifta*) him, and quieted my doubts and apprehensions. Still I was anxious to be kind and considerate to him, and to cure him of his ridiculous notions; but it was all in vain. At length he concocted a scheme with his abettors, and on the night of the 20th Zí-l hijja, he represented that he was going to visit the tomb of my father. Fifty horsemen in his interest came into the fort of Ágra, and went off in that direction. A little afterwards, intelligence was brought that Khusrú had

---

[1] [This account of Khusrú's rebellion has been translated by the Editor. It is the Emperor's own version of this important episode of his reign, and it will afford the means of comparing the two different versions of his Memoirs. See the account of the same transaction from the other version, *suprá*, p. 264.]

escaped. The *Amíru-l umará* having ascertained the fact, sent into my private apartments, desiring to speak with me on an urgent affair. I thought that perhaps some news had come from the Dakhin or from Gujarát. When I heard what had occurred, I said, "What is to be done, shall I mount and pursue him, or shall I send Khurram?" The *Amíru-l umará* said he would go if I would give him permission, and I said, "Be it so." He then said, "If he will not be persuaded to return, and force becomes necessary, what am I to do?" I said, "If he will not return to the right way without fighting, do not consider what you may do as a fault—sovereignty does not regard the relation of father and son, and it is said, a king should deem no one his relation." After having spoken these words, and settled some other matters, I sent him off. It then came to my recollection, that Khusrú had a great hatred of him. He (the *Amíru-l umará*) also, in consequence of the position and dignity that he holds, is envious of his peers, God forbid lest he should be malicious and destroy him! So I sent to call him back, and I despatched Shaikh Faríd Bokhárí on the service, directing him to take all the *mansabdárs* and *ahadís* he could collect. I determined that I myself would start as soon as it was day. * * The news came in that Khusrú was pressing forward to the Panjáb, but the thought came to my mind that he might perhaps be doing this as a blind, his real intention being to go elsewhere. Rájá Mán Singh, who was in Bengal, was Khusrú's maternal uncle, and many thought Khusrú would proceed thither. But the men who had been sent out in all directions confirmed the report of his going towards the Panjáb.

Next morning I arose, and placing my reliance on God, I mounted and set off, not allowing myself to be detained by any person or anything. When I reached the tomb of my honoured father, which is about three *kos* distant, I offered up prayers for the aid of his protecting spirit. Mirzá Hasan, son of Sháh Rukh Mirzá, who had formed the design of joining Khusrú, was brought in. I questioned him, but he denied the intention. I ordered them to bind his hands, and carry him back on an elephant. This capture I took as a good omen of the blessed assistance vouchsafed to me by that departed spirit.

At mid-day, when it became hot, I rested under the shade of some trees, and I observed to Khán-i 'azam, that I had been so engrossed with this unhappy matter that I had not taken the allowance of opium I usually took in the fore-part of the day, and that no one had reminded me of it. My distress arose from the thought that my son, without any cause or reason, had become my enemy, and that if I did not exert myself to capture him, dissatisfied and turbulent men would support him, or he would of his own accord go off to the Uzbeks or Kazilbáshes, and thus dishonour would fall upon my throne. Determined on the course to be pursued, after a short rest, I started from the *pargana* of Mathurá, which is twenty *kos* from A'gra, and after travelling two *kos* farther, I halted at one of the villages of that *pargana*, in which there was a tank.

When Khusrú arrived at Mathurá, he met Hasan Beg Khán Badakhshí, who had received favours from my father, and was coming from Kábul to wait upon me. The Badakhshís are by nature quarrelsome and rebellious, and when Khusrú, with his two or three hundred men, fell in with him, Khusrú made him commander of his men.[1] Every one whom they met on the road they plundered, and took from him his horse or goods. Merchants and travellers were pillaged, and wherever these insurgents went, there was no security for the women and children. Khusrú saw with his own eyes that a cultivated country was being wasted and oppressed, and their atrocities made people feel that death was a thousand times preferable. The poor people had no resource but to join them. If fortune had been at all friendly to him, he would have been overwhelmed with shame and repentance, and would have come to me without the least apprehension. It is well known how I pardoned his offences, and with what great kindness and gentleness I treated him, so as to leave no ground

[1] A very involved and obscure passage.

for suspicion in his breast. When, during the days of my father, he was incited by designing men to entertain improper aspirations, he knew that the fact had been communicated to me, but he showed no trust in my kindness.

His mother even, in the days when I was a prince, being grieved by his very unseemly acts, and by the unkindness of her younger brother Mádhu Singh, took poison and died.[1] How can I describe her excellences and good nature! She had an excellent understanding, and her affection for me was such that she would have given a thousand sons or brothers as a ransom for one hair of mine. She frequently wrote to Khusrú, and urged upon him the proofs of my kindness and affection, but it was all without effect; and when she found that there was no knowing to what lengths he would go, her Rájpút pride was wounded, and she set her heart upon death. From time to time her mind wandered, and her father and brothers all agreed in telling me she was insane. After a time she appeared to recover, but on the 26th Zí-l hijja, 1013 H., when I had gone out hunting, she, in a state of aberration, took an excessive quantity of opium, and died soon afterwards, hoping that her fate would bring her undutiful son to contrition. She was my first bride, and I was married to her in youth. After the birth of Khusrú, I gave her the title of Sháh Begam. Unable to endure the ill-conduct of her son and brothers towards me, she gave up her life, and so relieved herself from vexation and sorrow. Her death took such an effect upon me that I did not care to live, and had no pleasure in life. For four nights and days, that is for thirty-two watches, in the depth of distress and sorrow, I did not care to eat or drink. When my father heard of my state, in his extreme kindness and affection, he sent me a robe and the turban which he had worn upon his own head. This great favour fell like water on the flaming fire of my affliction, and gave me relief and comfort. But the recital of all this had no effect upon Khusrú. By his wicked and unfilial conduct he had caused the death of

[1] [See *suprá*, p. 112.]

his mother, and for no reason, but from mere freak and vicious fancy, he had broken out in rebellion against me, and thrown off all duty and obedience. It was necessary to punish his evil conduct, and at last he carried matters to such a length that he was placed in confinement.

On the 2nd Zí-l hijja I halted at Hindal, and sent Shaikh Faríd Bokhárí with some men in pursuit of Khusrú, and I gave him the command of the advance force. I sent Dost Muhammad to take care of Ágra, and of the palaces and treasure. When I departed from Ágra, I left that city in charge of 'Itimádu-d daula and Wazíru-l Mulk. I now told Dost Muhammad that as I was going to the Panjáb, and that province was under the *diwání* of 'Itimádu-d daula, he was to send the latter to me, and that he was to seize and keep in confinement the sons of Mirzá Muhammad Hakím, who were in Ágra; for if my own son could act in the way he had done, what might I expect from my uncle's sons? After the departure of Dost Muhammad, Mu'izzu-l Mulk became *bakhshí*.

I halted at Palol and Farídábád, and on the 13th reached Dehlí. There I visited the tomb of my grandfather Humáyún, and distributed alms to the poor. Then I went to the tomb of Nizámu-d dín Auliyá, and there also I had my bounty dispensed among the poor and needy. On the 14th Ramazán, I halted at the *sarái* of Naríla. Khusrú had set fire to this *sarái*, and then passed on. * * On the 16th I halted in the *pargana* of Pánípat, a place which had always been a fort unate one for my ancestors, and where two important victories had been won by them : one, the victory gained by Bábar over Ibráhím Lodí ; the other, the victory over Hímú by my honoured father. When Khusrú left Dehlí and got to Pánípat, it happened that Diláwar Khán had reached that place. The Khán received a short warning of his approach, and immediately sent his sons over the Jumna, while he pressed forward to throw himself into the fortress of Lahore before Khusrú could arrive there. About the same time, 'Abdu-r Rahím arrived from Lahore at the same place. Diláwar Khán advised him to send his sons over the river in the company of Diláwar's own sons, and himself to await my arrival. He was alarmed and timid; he could not resolve upon this course: but he delayed till Khusrú arrived, and then he waited upon him and joined him.

Diláwar Khán bravely pushed on towards Lahore. On his way he informed every Government servant, and every *krorí* merchant or other traveller he met, of the rebellion of Khusrú. Some he took with him, and some he warned to keep out of the way. After this the people were saved from the violence of the rebels. It seems very probable that, if Saiyid Kamál in Dehlí, and Diláwar Khán at Pánípat, had shown any vigour, and had thrown themselves in the way of Khusrú, the disorderly party which accompanied him would have been unable to make any resistance, and would have broken up, when Khusrú would have been taken prisoner. Their courage did not serve them on this occasion, but both of them made up for the deficiency afterwards.

Diláwar Khán, by rapid marching, reached Lahore before Khusrú, and exerted himself to put the fortress in a state of defence to repel the rebel. Kamál also had done his best to stop the rebel, as will be noticed in its proper place. On the 18th Zí-l hijja I reached Karnál, where I halted. * * On the 19th I stopped at Sháhábád, where there was great scarcity of water; but a heavy rain now fell, and gladdened every one. * * At Aloda I sent Abú-l Bani Uzbek with fifty-seven *mansabdárs* to the support of Shaikh Faríd, and I also sent by them 40,000 rupees for expenses. Seven thousand were given to Jamíl Beg, to pay arrears, and I also gave 18,000 to Mír Sharíf A'malí.

On the 24th Zí-l hijja five of Khusrú's followers were captured and brought in. Two of them who had entered into his service I ordered to be cast before elephants; the other three denied having undertaken to serve him, and they were placed under restraint till the truth could be ascertained. * * On the 24th Farwardín, a messenger arrived from Diláwar Khán to inform me that Khusrú was threatening Lahore, and to warn me to be cautious. On that same day the gates of Lahore were closed and secured, and two days afterwards Diláwar Khán entered the fortress with a few men. He immediately began to strengthen the place, repairing damages, mounting guns on the ramparts, and making all preparations for a siege. There was but a small force of troops in the place, but they were earnest, and had been appointed to their respective posts. The men of the city also were loyal and zealous.

Two days afterwards, when the preparations were complete, Khusrú arrived before the city, and commenced operations. He directed his followers to burn one of the gates in any way they could, and he promised them that after the capture of the fortress the place should be given up to plunder for seven days, and that the women and children should be their prisoners. The desperate villains set fire to one of the gates, but Diláwar Khán and the other officers inside the walls raised up another barrier [1] at the gate. Sa'íd Khán, who was encamped on the Chináb, being informed of these movements, marched rapidly to Lahore. On reaching the river Ráví, he informed the garrison of his presence, and requested them to find a means of bringing him into the fortress. They sent twenty boats, and brought him and some of his followers in.

On the ninth day of the siege Khusrú was informed of the approach of the Imperial army in pursuit of him and his adherents. Having no resource, he deemed it desirable to encounter the royal forces. Lahore is one of the largest cities in Hindústán, and in the course of six or seven days a great number of men had been got together. I had been well informed that 10,000 or 12,000 men were ready to march away from Lahore, and to make a night attack on the van of my army. This intelligence reached me on the night of the 16th, in the garden of Ágha Kulí. On the night of the 20th, although it was raining heavily, I marched, and on the following morning reached Sultánpúr. I remained

---

[1] [A doubtful word. Two MSS. have محازي, another يخراري, and a fourth leaves a blank.]

there till mid-day, and just at that time a great action began
between the royal army and the rebels. Mu'izzu-l Mulk had
just brought me some food, and I was about to enjoy myself,
when the news of the battle reached me. Directly I heard it,
although I had a very good appetite, I merely swallowed a
mouthful for good luck, and then mounted. Aware of the small-
ness of the force engaged, and anxious to bring up my men, I
determined to press on with all speed night and day. I called
for my great coat, but nobody brought it, and the only arms I
had were a javelin and sword. Confiding myself to the favour
of God, I started without hesitation. At first my escort did
not exceed fifty horse, and no one knew that a battle was on that
day imminent. At the bridge of Govindwál my men numbered
four or five hundred, good and bad. After crossing the bridge,
intelligence of victory reached me. The man who brought it
was an officer of the wardrobe named Shamshír, and to him I
gave the title of Khush-khabr Khán. Mír Jamálu-d dín, whom
I had before sent to warn Khusrú, arrived just at the same time,
and he spoke so much about the numbers and strength of Khusrú,
that my men were frightened, until the news of victory was confirmed by successive messengers. This Saiyid was a simple
fellow. He would not believe the report, but expressed his
incredulity that an army such as he had seen could have been
vanquished by so small and unprepared a force as that of Shaikh
Faríd. But when the litter of Khusrú was brought in attended
by two eunuchs, he then believed, and alighting from his horse,
he placed his head at my feet, and offered his congratulations.

Shaikh Faríd had acted in this battle with the greatest zeal
and fidelity. He placed the Saiyids of Bárha, the heroes of the
age, in the advance; and they fought most bravely. Saif Khán,
son of Saiyid Mahmúd Khán, the chief of the tribe, greatly
distinguished himself, and received eighteen wounds. Saiyid
Jalál, another of the tribe, received an arrow in the head, and
died in a few days. The Saiyids of Bárha in this action did
not exceed fifty or sixty in number. These Saiyids repulsed

the attack of 1000 horse and 500 Badakhshís, and were cut to pieces. Saiyid Kamál, with his brothers, was sent to support the advanced force, and he attacked the enemy vigorously in flank. The right wing, shouting, "Long live the King!" bore down, and the enemy, stricken with panic, broke and fled in all directions. Nearly 400 of the enemy were killed, and Khusrú's chest of jewels and trinkets, which he always carried with him, was captured. * *

I placed Mahábat Khán and 'Alí Beg Akbarsháhí in command of a force to pursue Khusrú wherever he should go. I also determined that if he went to Kábul, I would follow him, and not return till I had got him into my hands. If he should not stay in Kábul, but go off to Badakhshán and those parts, I would leave Mahábat Khán in Kábul, and follow him thither, lest he might ally himself to the Uzbeks, and bring disgrace to my throne. * *

On the 28th my camp rested at Jahán, seven _kos_ from Lahore. On that day Khusrú came with a few followers to the banks of the Chináb. After his defeat, the opinions of those who escaped with him differed. The Afgháns and the Hindústánís, who were mostly his oldest adherents, wished to turn back to Hindústán, and there raise disturbances. Husain Beg, whose wives and children and treasure were in the direction of Kábul, was in favour of going towards Kábul. When he resolved upon the latter course, the Afgháns and Hindústánís separated from him. Upon reaching the Chináb, he wanted to cross at Sháhpúr, one of the regular ferries; but as he could not get boats, he went to the ferry of Súdhara. There they found one boat without boatmen, and another boat made of wood and straw. Before the defeat of Khusrú, an order had been issued to all the _jágirdárs_, road-keepers, and ferrymen of the Panjáb, informing them of what had happened, and warning them to be careful. In consequence of this notice, the ferries and rivers were watched. Husain Beg was about to take the two boats and send Khusrú over. But just at this juncture, a _chaudharí_ of Súdhara came up, and saw

that a party of men were going to cross over the river by night.
He expostulated with the boatmen of the wood and straw boat,
and told them that the Emperor's order was, that no boat should
pass over by night. The contention and noise brought a number
of men together, and the boat was taken away from the boatmen,
and no one would convey them over. Abú-l Kásim Khán, who
had charge of the ferry at Gujarát, when he was informed that a
party of men wanted to cross the Chináb, proceeded to the place
with his sons and some horsemen. Husain Jeg * * got four
boats, and attempted to cross; but the last one stuck on a sand-
bank. At daybreak Abú-l Kásim and Khwája Khizr, who was
director of the boatmen, assembled a party and secured the
western bank of the river. The eastern bank was occupied by
the *zamíndárs*. A force which I had sent under Sa'íd Khán
now came up at a most opportune time, and assisted to capture
Khusrú. On the 29th of the month, men riding on elephants
and in boats secured him. Next day I heard of his capture,
and I immediately sent the *Amíru-l umará* to bring Khusrú to
my presence. In matters of Government and State it frequently
happens that one has to act upon one's own judgment. Of the
councils I have held, there are two which are remarkable. First,
when, in opposition to the counsel of all my friends, I left Allahábád, and went to wait upon my father, through which I obtained
his pardon, and became King. Second, when I resolved instantly
to pursue Khusrú, and not to rest till I had taken him. * * On
the 3rd of Muharram, 1015 A.H., Khusrú was brought into my
presence in the garden of Mirzá Kámrán, with his hands bound
and a chain on his leg, and he was led up from the left side,
according to the rule of Changíz Khán. Husain Beg was on his
right, and 'Abdu-l 'Azíz on his left; he stood between them,
trembling and weeping. Husain Beg, suspecting that they
would make a scape-goat of him, began to speak sorrowfully, but
they did not allow him to continue. I gave Khusrú into custody,
and I ordered these two villains to be inclosed in the skins of
a cow and an ass, and to be placed on asses, face to the tail, and

so to be paraded round the city. As the skin of a cow dries quicker than the skin of an ass, Husain Beg lived only to the fourth watch, and then died. 'Abdu-l 'Azíz, who was in the ass's skin, and had moisture conveyed to him,[1] survived.

From the last day of Zí-l hijja till the 9th Muharram, in consequence of bad weather, I remained in the garden of Mirzá Kámrán. I attributed the success gained in this expedition to Shaikh Faríd, and I dignified him with the title of Murtazá Khán. To strengthen and confirm my rule, I directed that a double row of stakes should be set up from the garden to the city, and that the rebel *awaimáks*,[2] and others who had taken part in this revolt, should be impaled thereon, and thus receive their deserts in this most excruciating punishment. The land-holders between the Chináb and Behat who had proved their loyalty, I rewarded by giving to each one of them some lands as *madad-ma'ásh*. * *

The disposal of Khusrú still remained unsettled. As the vicinity of A'gra was a hot-bed of disaffection, I was desirous that it should be cleared of dangerous persons, lest these pretensions of Khusrú should be backed up and kept alive. So I directed my son Parwez to leave several *sardárs* to carry on the campaign against the Ráná, and to proceed himself with A'saf Khán and 200 others to A'gra, and there to undertake the control and protection of the city. But before they arrived there, Khusrú's attempt had been crushed to the satisfaction of my friends, so I directed Parwez to come and meet me. On the 9th Muharram I entered Lahore. My friends and well-wishers advised me to return to A'gra, because Gujarát, the Dakhin, and Bengal were all in a disordered state. But this advice did not approve itself to me, because I had learnt from the letters of Sháh Beg Khán,

---

[1] [" In the excess of his impudence he drew a dog's skin over his face (*i.e.* he acted like a dog), and as he was led through the streets and bázárs, he ate cucumbers and anything else containing moisture that fell into his hands. He survived the day and night. Next day the order was given for taking him out of the skin. There were many maggots in his skin, but he survived it all."—*Ikbál-náma*.]

[2] [See *supra*, p. 267.]

the ruler of Kandahár, sundry facts all tending to show that the
amirs of the frontier of the Kazilbáshes had designs upon
Kandahár. * * Intelligence reached me at Lahore, that the
Kazilbáshes had inclosed the fort of Kandahár on three sides,
and it was evident that further delay would be dangerous; so I
sent a force thither under the command of Ghází Beg Khán and
* * *. With a view to prevent the threatened danger, I determined to proceed to Kábul, and to postpone my proposed
excursion round about Lahore.]

Second Year of the Reign.

[The second new year of my auspicious reign began on the
22nd Zí-l ka'da, 1015 a.h. (10th March, 1603 a.d.).]

Journey to Kábul.

On the 7th of Zí-l hijja, at a prosperous hour, I left the fort
of Lahore, and crossing the Rávi, alighted at the garden of Díl-
ámez, and stopped there for four days. I passed Sunday, the
19th of Farwardín, which was the day of the Sun's entry into
Aries, in that garden. Some of my servants were favoured with
promotion. Ten thousand rupees in cash were given to Husain
Beg, the ambassador of the ruler of Írán. I left Kalij Khán,
Míran Sadr-jahán, and Mír Sharíf A´malí at Lahore, and authorized them to conduct all transactions in concert with each other.
On Monday I marched from the garden to the village called
Harípúr, three and a half *kos* from the city. On Tuesday,
my flags waved in Jahángírpúr, which was a hunting-ground of
mine. Near this village a minaret was raised by my orders over
an antelope of mine, called "Ráj," which was not only the best
fighter in my possession, but was the best decoy for wild ones.
Mullá Muhammad Husain of Kashmir, who in caligraphy ex-
celled all persons of his profession, had engraved the following
words on a piece of stone: "In this delightful spot an antelope
was caught by the Emperor Núru-d dín Muhammad Jahángír,

which in the space of a month became entirely tame, and was considered the best of all the royal antelopes." Out of regard to this animal I ordered that no one should hunt antelopes in this for· t, and that their flesh should be considered as unlawful as that of a cow to the infidel Hindús, and as that of a hog to the Musulmáns. The stone of its tomb was carved into the shape of a deer. I ordered Sikandaı Maí, the *jágirdár* of the *pargana*, to erect a fort in Jahángírpúr.

On Thursday, the 14th, we encamped in the *pargana* of Chand-wála, and, after one intervening stage, arrived on Saturday at Háfizábád, and put up in the buildings erected under the super-intendence of Mír Kiránu-d dín, who held the office of *krorí* at that station. In two marches more I reached the banks of the Chináb.

On Thursday, the 21st Zí-l hijja, I crossed the river over a bridge of boats, and pitched my tents in the *pargana* of Gujarát. When the Emperor Akbar was proceeding to Kashmír, he built a fort on the other side of the river, and made the Gújars, who had been hitherto devoted to plunder, dwell there. The place was consequently named Gujarát, and formed into a separate *pargana*. The Gújars live chiefly upon milk and curds, and seldom cultivate land.

On Friday we arrived at Khawáspúr, five *kos* from Gujarát, which was peopled by Khawás Khán, a servant of Sher Khán Pathán. Beyond it, after two marches, we reached the banks of the Behat, and pitched our tents there. In the night a very strong wind blew, dark clouds obscured the sky, and it rained so heavily that even the oldest persons had never seen such rain within their memory. The rain ended with showers of hail-stones, which were as large as hens' eggs. The torrent of water and the wind combined broke the bridge. I with my ladies crossed the river in a boat, and as there were but very few boats for the other men to embark on, I ordered that they should wait till the bridge was repaired, which was accomplished in a week, when the whole camp crossed the river without any trouble.

The source of the river Behat is a fountain in Kashmír,
called Vírnág.   The name signifies in the Hindí language
a snake, and it appears that at one time a very large snake
haunted the spot.   I visited this source twice during the lifetime of my father.   It is about twenty *kos* from the city of
Kashmír.   The spring rises in a basin, of an octangular form,
about twenty yards in length, by twenty in breadth.   The
vestiges of the abodes of devotees, numerous chambers made of
stone, and caves, are in the neighbourhood.   Its water is so clear
that although its depth is said to be beyond estimation, yet if a
poppy-seed be thrown in, it will be visible till it reaches the bottom.
There are very fine fish in it.   As I was told that the fountain was
unfathomably deep, I ordered a stone to be tied to the end of a
rope and thrown into it, and thus it was found that its depth did
not exceed the height of a man and a half.   After my accession,
I ordered its sides to be paved with stones, a garden to be made
round it, and the stream which flowed from it to be similarly
decorated on both sides.   Such elegant chambers and edifices
were raised on each side of the basin, that there is scarcely anything to equal it throughout the inhabited world.[1]   The river
expands much when it reaches near the village of Pampúr, which
is ten *kos* from the city.

All the saffron of Kashmír is the product of this village.
Perhaps there is no other place in the world where saffron
is so abundantly produced : the quantity annually yielded
there being 500 *maunds* of Hindústán, or 4000 *maunds* of
Kábul (*wiláyat*).   I visited this place once with my father in
the season in which the plant blossoms.   In all other trees
we see they first get the branches, then the leaves, and after
all the flower.   But it is otherwise with this plant.   It blossoms
when it is only about two inches high from the ground.
Its flower is of a bluish colour, having four leaves and four
threads of orange colour, like those of safflower, in length equal

[1] Compare Forster's *Journal*, vol. ii. p. 4 ; Von Hügel's *Kaschmir*, vol. i. p. 291 ;
Vigne's *Kashmir*, vol. i. p. 333 ; Moorcroft's *Travels*, vol. ii. p. 250.

to one joint of the finger. The fields of saffron are sometimes
a *kos*, sometimes half a *kos* in length, and they look very beautiful at a distance. In the season when it is collected, it has
such a strong smell that people get headache from it. Although
I had taken a glass of wine, yet I was also affected by it. I
asked the Kashmirians, who were employed in collecting it,
whether it took any effect upon them, and was surprised by the
reply, which was, "they did not know even what the headache
was."

The stream that flows from the fountain of Vírnág is called
Behat in Kashmír, and becomes a large river, when it is
joined by many other smaller ones on both sides. It runs
through the city. In some places its breadth does not exceed
the reach of an arrow shot from a bow. Nobody drinks its
water, because it is very dirty and unwholesome. All people
drink from a tank called Dal, which is near the city. The river
Behat, after falling into this tank, takes its course through
Bárah-Múlah, Pakalí, and Damtaur, and then enters the Panjáb.
There are many rivulets and fountains in Kashmír, but Darah-
lár, which joins the Behat at the village of Shahábu-d dínpúr,
is the best of all the streams.

This village is one of the most famous places in Kashmír;
and in it, in a piece of verdant land, there are nearly a
hundred handsome planę trees, the branches of which inter-
lace and afford a deep and extensive shade. The surface of
the land is so covered with green that it requires no carpet to
be spread on it. The village was founded by Sultán Zainu-l
'Ábidín, who ruled firmly over Kashmír for fifty-two years.
He is called there Barosháh, or the Great King. He is said
to have performed many miracles. The remains of his many
buildings are still to be seen there; and among these there
is a building called Barín[1] Lanká, which he built with great
difficulty in the middle of the lake called Ulur (Wulur), about

---

[1] [The *Tabakát-i Akbarí* calls it Zain-lanká. *Suprà*, Vol. V. p. 465.]

three or four *kos* in circumference. This lake is exceedingly
deep. To form the foundation of the building, boat-loads of
stone were thrown into the lake; but as this proved of no
use, some thousands of boats laden with stones were sunk,
and so with great labour a foundation of a hundred yards
square was raised above the water, and smoothed. On one
side of it were erected a palace and a place for the worship
of God, than which no finer buildings can anywhere be found.
Generally he used to come to this place in a boat, and devoted
his time there to the worship of Almighty God. It is said
that he passed many periods of forty days in this place.

One day one of his sons came into the sacred place, with
a drawn sword in his hand, with the intention of killing him.
But as soon as his eye fell upon him, the natural affection
of the son and the royal dignity of the parent struck him
with dismay, and diverted him from his purpose. After a short
time the King came out, and having embarked in the same boat
with his son, returned towards the city. Midway he told his
son that he had left behind him his rosary, and asked him to
return in a skiff and bring it to him. When the Prince went
back to the building, he was amazed to find the King also there.
He was exceedingly sorry for what he had done, and immediately fell at his feet, soliciting forgiveness for his conduct.

The King is said to have performed many such miracles, and
that he could assume any form he liked. Reflecting on the
habits and manners of his sons, and knowing that they were
very impatient and anxious to ascend the throne, he told them
that with him it was easy to resign the crown and to die, but
that they could do nothing after him, for their government
would not last long, and but few days would elapse before they
would see the reward of their conduct. Having said this, he
left off eating and drinking, and passed forty days in the same
manner. He did not even doze during this interval of time, but
like a great saint he directed his whole attention to the worship
of the Omnipotent God. On the fortieth day he delivered his

soul to the angel of death, and met with the mercy of his Maker.

He left three sons, viz. A'dam Khán, Hájí Khán, and Bahrám Khán. They quarrelled among themselves, and at last lost the dominions of their father. The sovereignty of Kashmír fell into the hands of a class called Chaks, who were formerly but common soldiers. Three rulers of this tribe constructed three buildings on the remaining three faces of the foundation which was laid by Zainu-l 'A'bidín in the lake of Ulur, but none of them is so substantial as the first one built by that King.

Kashmír is a delightful country in the seasons of autumn and spring. I visited it in the former season, and found it even more charming than I had anticipated. I never was there in spring, but I hope some time or other to be there during that season.

[1] On Saturday, the 1st of Muharram, I marched from the bank of the Behat to Rohtás, with one stage intervening. The fort of Rohtás is one of the buildings of Sher Khán Afghán, and is constructed amongst the ravines, where it was scarcely conceivable that so strong a position could have been obtained. As this tract is near the country of the Gakkhurs, a troublesome and turbulent race, it came into his head to build this fort for the purpose of overawing and controlling them. Sher Khán died when only a portion of the work was done, but it was completed by his son Salím Khán. Over one of the doors the cost of the fort is engraven on a stone, which is set in the wall. The amount is 16,10,00,000 *dáms* and something more, which is 34,25,000 rupees of Hindústán,[2] 120,000 *túmáns* of I'rán, or 1,21,75,000 *khánis* of Túrán.

On Tuesday, the 4th, I marched four *kos* and three-quarters to Tillah,[3] which means "a hill" in the Gakkhur language.

---

[1] [Sir H. M. Elliot's own translation.]

[2] It is worth bearing this comparatively moderate estimate in mind, for our modern travellers rarely place it under 100,00,000, and one has it as high as 500,00,000 rupees.

[3] The original reads *Bilah*, but *Tillah* must be meant, which bears the meaning ascribed, and though the lofty Tillah cannot itself be meant, yet the halting ground is sufficiently close to admit of its deriving its name from that conspicuous hill.

From that place I marched to the village of Bhakra,[1] which in the language of the same people is the name of a shrub with white flowers without any odour. From Tillah to Bhakra I marched the whole way through the bed of a river,[2] in which water was then flowing, and the oleander bushes were in full bloom, and of exquisite colour, like peach blossoms. In Hindústán this evergreen is always in flower. There were very many growing at the sides of this stream, and I ordered my personal attendants, both horse and foot, to bind bunches of the flowers in their turbans, and I directed that the turbans of those who would not decorate themselves in this fashion should be taken off their heads. I thus got up a beautiful garden.

On Thursday, the 6th, Hatyá[3] was the encamping ground. On this march a great many Palás[4] shrubs were found in blossom. This shrub is also peculiar to the jungles of Hindústán. It has no fragrance in its flowers, which are of a fiery orange colour. The trunk is black. The flowers are the size of a red rose, or even bigger. It was such a sight that it was impossible to take one's eyes off it. As the air was very charming, and as, in consequence of a veil of clouds obscuring the light of the sun, there was a slight shower, I indulged myself in drinking wine. In short, I enjoyed myself amazingly on this march.

---

[1] This is now called Bakrála, correctly Bekkrála. The local name for this flower is Phakra, elsewhere it is ordinarily called Haft-chingara. It is not more common at Bakrála than elsewhere in the neighbourhood, and I could get no one to acknowledge that this was, or could be, the origin of the name; so I suspect that the royal autobiographer has been deceived by his informants.

[2] This is the Káhan, a troublesome stream, full of quicksands.

[3] This is a few miles beyond the usual encamping ground at present, which is Dhamak, a most impracticable name of which to obtain the true pronunciation. In the village and by the same men I have heard it variously given as Damak, Dhamak, Damihak, Tam'ak, Tamiák, Tamihak, the *d.* and *t* being convertible in these parts, as "antá" for "andá," an egg. It was here that Shahábu-d din Ghori was assassinated, and in the lines which record the dates of his death, given in the *Lubbu-t Tawárikh*, the place is called Damyek. One of our road books (in the Bengal and Agra Guide) renders the confusion worse confounded, by attempting to be specific, and recording it as "Tamako, near Dhamack." Dhamak appears the most correct. The *zamindárs* are of the Awán tribe.

[4] Generally called "Dhák," *Butea frondosa.*

This place is called Hatyá because it was founded by a Gakkhur named Hátí. The country from Márgalla to Hatyá is called Pothúwár.[1] Within this tract there are but few crows to be found. Between Rohtás and Hatyá is the country of the Búgyáls,[2] who are of the same stock, and connected with the Gakkhurs.

On Friday I marched four *kos* and three-quarters to Pakka, so called because it has a *sarái* built of baked bricks; and Pakka in the Hindí language means "baked." There was nothing but dust on the road; and in consequence of the annoyances I experienced, I found it a very troublesome march. In this place most of the sorrel brought from Kábul got injured.

On Saturday, the 8th, I marched four and a half *kos* to a place called Khar, which means "broken ground" in the Gakkhur language.[3] This country is very bare of trees.[4]

On Sunday I pitched my camp on the other side of Ráwal Pindí, so called because it was founded by a Hindú named Ráwal, and Pindí[5] in that language means "a village." Near this place there is a stream of flowing water in a ravine, which

[1] It is so called now, or rather Pathwár, but the pronunciation is not distinct, Various origins are ascribed to the name, none of them satisfactory. One is, that Phútwár is the proper name, on account of the mixed tribes which this table-land contains, in consequence of the frequent depopulation it has undergone. Another, that when it was under Kashmír, the collections used to be carried there in bags, called *pithú*. Another, because the land is *patwár*, or level between the hills which form its boundaries. There are tracts in India, as those under the Siudian and Sulaimáni Hills, called Pát, for this reason; but the ground here can only be called level by comparison, for it is intersected by ravines in every direction, and this very fact is assigned as another origin of the name, the soil being *phútwár*, or broken. As this is conspicuously the case all the way from Dhamak to Márgalla, I am disposed to look on this as the most probable origin, though the present pronunciation omits the aspirate with the *p*.

[2] This tract is now called Bágyál from the Gakkhur tribe of that name, descendants of Sultán Búgá.

[3] Spelt "Kor" in the original, but Khor must be meant, as it bears the meaning ascribed to it in the text, though there is no village of that name. The present encamping ground is Mánikyála, where is the celebrated Buddhist tope, of which it is surprising that Jahángír makes no mention.

[4] A later traveller, speaking of this country, says truly, "I never passed through a country so devoid of any pretension to beauty."—Baron Hügel's *Travels*, p. 238.

[5] It can scarcely be called Hindí. It prevails throughout the Panjáb, but is unknown to the east of the Jumna.

empties itself into a tank. As the place was not destitute of charms, I remained there for a short time. I asked the Gakkhurs what the depth of the water was. They gave no specific answer, and added, "We have heard from our fathers that there are alligators in this water, which wound and kill every animal that goes into it, and on this account no one dares enter it." I ordered a sheep to be thrown into the water, which swam round the whole tank, and came out safe. After that I ordered a swimmer to go in, and he also emerged safe. It was therefore evident that there was no foundation for what the Gakkhurs asserted. The breadth of this water is about a bow-shot.

On Monday I encamped at Kharbuza. The Gakkhurs in former days erected a domed structure here, in which they used to collect tolls from travellers. As the dome is in shape like a melon, it was called Kharbuza.

On Tuesday, the 11th, the camp moved to Kálá-pání, which means in Hindí "black water." On this march there occurs a hill called Márgalla.[1] _Már_, in Hindí, signifies "to rob on the highway," and _galla_, "a caravan,"—that is, it is a place where caravans are plundered. Up to this extends the boundary of the country of the Gakkhurs. These fellows are strange animals, always squabbling and fighting with one another. I did all I could to effect a reconciliation, but without effect. "The life of fools is held very cheap in troublous times."

On Wednesday, our encamping ground was Bábá Hasan Abdál. About a _kos_ to the east of this place there is a cascade, over which the water flows with great rapidity. On the whole road to Kábul there is no stream like this, but on the road to Kashmír thence are two or three of the same kind. Rájá Mán Singh raised a small edifice in the middle of the basin whence the water flows. There are several fish in it, of half or a quarter

---

[1] The road has been improved since this Emperor's time. There is a substantial stone pavement through the pass, which from a Persian inscription on a rock appears to have been erected in A.H. 1084, by "the strong-handed Khán Mahábat Shikoh."

of a yard long. I stayed three days at this charming spot, and drank wine with my intimate companions. I also had some sport in the way of fishing. I had never, up to this time thrown the *Safra* net, which in Hindí they call " *Bhanwar Jál,*' and is one of the commonest kind. To throw this net is a matter of some difficulty, but I tried it with my own hand, and succeeded in getting twelve fish. I strung pearls in their noses, and let them go again in the water. I asked the inhabitants and people acquainted with history who Bábá Hasan Abdál was, but no one could give me any specific information. The most noted spot there is where a spring issues from the foot of the hill. It is exceedingly pure and clear, and the following verse of Mír Khusrú may well be applied to it. "The water is so transparent, that a blind man in the depth of night could see the small particles of sand at the bottom." Khwája Shamsu-d dín Khwáfí, who was for a long time the minister of my respected father, erected a small summer-house there,[1] and excavated a cistern into which the water of the spring flows, supplying the fields and gardens with the means of irrigation. Close to it he built a domed tomb for himself, but it was not his fate to be buried there. Hakím Abú-l Fath Gílání and his brother Hakím Humám, who were the most intimate friends of my father, and to whom he entrusted all his secrets, were buried there by his orders.[2]

On the 15th I encamped at Amardí, a most extraordinary green plain, in which you cannot see a mound or hillock of any kind. At this place and in the neighbourhood there are seven

[1] It is probable that this is the place now occupied by Sikh Granthis, who have set up there the *panja*, or hand, of Bábá Nának, and have established the cistern as a sacred spot where they feed fat fish. Considering at what a late period this place came under the dominion of the Sikhs, it is curious that popular feeling should concur in the new belief that Bábá Nának visited the spot and performed the miracle ascribed to him, which is recorded by our modern travellers who have visited the spot.

[2] There is an old tomb in this situation, now domeless, which is no doubt the place indicated. The inhabitants say some prince is buried there, some say Núr Jahán Begam, but she is buried not far from Jahángír, at Sháhderah, in an elegant structure like a *bárádarí* (summer-house), now falling rapidly to ruin.

or eight thousand houses of Khaturs and Dilazáks, who practise
every kind of turbulence, oppression, and highway robbery. I
gave orders that the *sarkár* of Attak, as well as this tract of
country, should be made over to Zafar Khán, the son of Zain
Khán Koka, and I gave him directions, that before the return of
the royal camp from Kábul, he should march off the whole of
the Dilazáks towards Lahore, and should seize the chiefs of the
Khaturs, and keep them in prison and fetters.[1]

On Monday, the 17th, I encamped near the fort of Attak,[2]
on the banks of the river Níláb, after making one march interme-
diately. At this place I promoted Mahábat Khán to the rank
of 2500. This fort, which is very strong, was constructed under
the direction and superintendence of Khwája Shamsu-d dín
Khwáfí by order of my father. In these days the Níláb was
very full, insomuch that the bridge consisted of eighteen boats,
over which people passed with great ease and security. The
Amíru-l Umará was so weak and sick, that I left him at Attak,
and as the country around Kábul was not able to subsist so large

[1] His orders appear to have been faithfully executed, for there are now no
Dilazáks here. There are some in Hazára, who call themselves Turks. Of the
Khaturs there are still several villages, such as Wáke, Kate, etc., and the fertile
plain of Khatur is still called after their name. They called themselves Mughals,
and also say they were converted Itájpúts, whose original seat was Dehlí. Others say
their name is owing to their being converted Khattris, others because they practise
agriculture (*khetí*). The little information which the people of this neighbourhood
can give about themselves is as remarkable now as in Jahángír's time. Of the
Dilazáks Elphinstone says :—" All the lower valley of the Caubul, all the plain of
Peshawer, with part of Bajour, Chush Huzaurah, and the countries east of them,
as far as the Hydaspes, belonged to the Afghaun tribe of Dilazauk, which is now
almost extirpated. The country between the Dilazauks and the range of Hindoo
Coosh on both sides of the Indus, formed the kingdom of Swaut, which was
inhabited by a distinct nation, and ruled by Sultán Oneiss, whose ancestors had long
reigned over that country. The Ghorees descended to Peshawer in the reign of
Cawmraun, the son of Baubar, and with the assistance of that prince drove the
Dilazauks across the Indus; of that numerous and powerful tribe, there are now
only two or three villages to the west of the Indus. There are, however, some
thousand Dilazauks on the Indian side of the river."—*Kingdom of Caubul*, vol. ii.
pp. 12, 56.

[2] At that period the place was called Attak Banáras, as it is now in the vicinity
of the place itself. [See *suprà*, Vol. V. p. 443.] Banáras is a small ruinous town,
about a mile to the east of the fort, where the tomb and garden of Bairám Beg, the
guardian of Akbar, are still conspicuous.

a camp as accompanied me, I ordered the *bakhshís* to allow no one to cross the river except my own friends and household; the main camp being ordered to wait at Attak till my return.

On Wednesday, the 19th, I embarked with the Prince and a few attendants on a raft, and passing over the Níláb [1] in safety, landed on the bank of the Káma,[2] the river which flows under Jalálábád. These rafts are composed of bamboos and grass, and placed on inflated skins. Here they call them *Jál*,[3] and in rivers where there are many stones, they are safer than boats.[4] I gave 12,000 rupees to Mír Sharíf Ámalí and the officers who were left on duty at Lahore, to be distributed to the poor; and orders were given to 'Abdu-r Razák M'amúrí and Bihárí Dás, paymaster of the Ahadís, to make arrangements for supplying with every necessary the party who had been left behind with Zafar Khán.

From that ground we moved, one march intervening, to my camp near Saráí Bára. On the opposite side of the river Káma there is a fort,[5] built by Zain Khán Koka, when he was appointed to exterminate the Yúsufzáí Afgháns. It is called Naushahra, and nearly 50,000 rupees were expended in its construction. They report that His Majesty Humáyún hunted wolves in these parts, and I have heard my father say, that he

[1] The river is not now known by this name, since the town of Níláb has declined, and Attak has risen. From the north-east downwards it is called Abbásín, and from Attak to Kálábágh, the Attals. By the Hindús of that neighbourhood it is frequently called the Sind, under which name they read of it in their Shásters.

[2] This name is derived from a fort nearly opposite Jalálabád, at the junction of the Kuner with the river which Englishmen call the Kábul river. The Kuner is also called the Káma; but the lower part of the Kábul river, which Jahángír calls the Káma, is now generally known as the Lundye, or Landa. The Lundye proper rises in the Panjkora country, and flows nearly due south into the Kábul river, opposite Peshawar. Lieut. Macartney says that the stream is called the Káma from Jalálábád as far as Peshawar.—Elphinstone's *Kingdom of Caubul*, vol. ii. p. 473.

[3] *Jál* is now the term.

[4] Any one who has tried these convenient floats can testify to this. In the upper rivers of the Panjáb an inverted bed is usually placed on two skins, and the float is then called *Kha-náo*, "a bed-boat."

[5] There is now a Naushahra on either side of the river. Near the town of the Yúsufzáí bank the Kála-pání enters the Lundye.

had himself attended his father two or three times on these excursions.

On Tuesday, the 25th, I moved to Sarái Daulatábád. Ahmad Beg Kábulí, the *jágírdár* of Pesháwar, brought the Yúsufzái and Ghoryá-khail chiefs with him to pay their respects. As I was not pleased with his services, I removed him from the government of that country, and bestowed it upon Sher Khán Afghán.

On Wednesday, the 26th, I arrived at the garden of Sardár Khán, near Pesháwar. Ghorkhatrí, a famous place of worship amongst the Jogís, is in this neighbourhood, and I went to see it in the possible chance of seeing some *fakír*, from whose society I might derive advantage; but such a man is as rare as the Philosopher's Stone or the 'Anká; and all that I saw was a small fraternity without any knowledge of God, the sight of whom filled my heart with nothing but regret.

On Thursday Jamrúd was our encamping ground.

On Friday we went through the Khaibar Pass, and encamped at 'Alí Masjid.[1] * * *

A Hindu Murderer.

On the same day (3rd Safar) Kaliyán, son of Rájá Bikramájít, arrived from Gujarát. Many heinous deeds of villany were reported of this mean and vicious character. One among his other atrocities is that he kept a common woman of the Muhammadan persuasion in his house, and for fear of being discovered, he killed her father and mother, and buried them in his house. I ordered him to be imprisoned until the facts were ascertained. After conviction I ordered that his tongue should be cut out,[2] that he should be kept in prison for life, and that he should be fed at the same mess as the dog-keepers and sweepers. * * *

---

[1] [End of Sir H. M. Elliot's translation. A note states that he deemed it unnecessary to carry the translation of this itinerary further.]

[2] [This excision of the tongue is not mentioned in some MSS.]

Bábar's Memoirs.

With the object of acquiring information about the history of
Kábul, I used to read the *Wáki'át-i Bábo 'i*, which, all except
four parts (*juzw*), was written with his (Bábar's) own hand. To
complete the work I copied these parts (*ajzá*) myself, and at the
end I added some paragraphs in the Turkish language, to show
that they were written by me. Although I was brought up in
Hindústán, yet I am not deficient in reading and writing Turkí.

Prince Khusrú.

On the 12th I summoned Khusrú to my presence, and ordered
the chains to be put off from his legs, and that he should be
allowed to walk in the garden of Shahr-árá, for my paternal affection had not so far departed as to induce me to deprive him of this
indulgence. * * * Although Khusrú had been repeatedly guilty
of improper actions, and was deserving of a thousand punishments, yet paternal affection did not allow me to take his life.
To bear with such wicked proceedings was incompatible with the
rules of government and policy; yet I overlooked his offences, and
he was kept in great comfort and ease. It was discovered that he
had sent people to several vile and wicked characters, and by promises had instigated them to raise disturbances, and to attempt
my life. Some of these wretched, shortsighted people conspired
together and formed the design of destroying me while engaged
in hunting at Kábul and its vicinity; but as the favour of Pro-
vidence is the protector and preserver of kings, they found no
opportunity to commit that crime. The day on which I halted
at Surkháb, one of the conspirators hastily came to Khwája
Kuraishí, the *díwán* of Prince Khurram, and said that about
500 insurgents, with Fathu-lla, son of Hakím Abú-l Fath,
Núru-d dín, son of Ghiyásu-d dín Alí, Ásaf Khán, and Sharíf,
son of I'timádu-d daula, were, at the instigation of Khusrú, on
the watch for a suitable opportunity of making an attack upon
me. The Khwájá immediately reported the matter to Khurram,

who in great perturbation instantly came and informed me. I blessed the Prince, and resolved to take measures for the apprehension of all those imprudent persons, and for treating them with every kind of severe punishment. But again I thought that as I was now on a journey, their pursuit would cause the disturbance and dispersion of my camp, and accordingly only the chief insurgents were captured. Fathu-lla Khán was placed in prison, in charge of some trustworthy persons, while the two other wretches, with three or four more ringleaders of those cursed revolters, were killed.

THIRD YEAR OF THE REIGN.

The third Nauroz after my happy accession to the throne occurred on Thursday, the 2nd of Zí-l hijja, corresponding with the 1st of Farwardín, and the world-enlightening Sun, after leaving the sign of Pisces, entered that of Aries. The festival of *Nauroz* was celebrated in the village of Rankata, which is at the distance of five *kos* from the city of Ágra. * * *

As the magnificent sepulchre of my father was on the road, I thought that if I now went to see it, ignorant people would consider that I went to visit it only because it was on my road. I therefore determined that I would proceed direct to the city, and then, as my father, in accordance with his vow respecting my birth, had gone on foot from Ágra to Ájmír, in the same manner I would also walk from the city to his splendid sepulchre, a distance of two and a half *kos*. Would that I could have gone this distance upon my head !

'n Saturday, the 5th of the month, at noon, in an auspicious hour, I set out towards the city. As I went, I distributed about 5000 rupees to the beggars, who lined both sides of the road along the whole way, till I entered my palace within the fort. On the same day, Rájá Nar Singh Deo brought to me a white leopard. Though among animals of other species, both quadrupeds and birds, there may be some of white colour, distinguished by the name of *towíghun*,[1] yet a white leopard I had never seen up to this time.

On Thursday, the 8th of Muharram, A.H. 1016, Jalálu-d dín Mas'úd, who held the rank of 400, and was not destitute of courage, and in several actions had shown valour which was more nearly allied to rashness, expired of dysentery at the age of between fifty and sixty years. He was much addicted to opium, and took it after breaking it into small pieces like cheese. He often received it from the hands of his mother. When his illness grew worse, and symptoms of death were visible, she took a large quantity of the same opium which she used to give him, and died a few minutes after he departed this world. To this time such maternal love for a son has never been heard of. It is a custom among the Hindús that women burn themselves alive after the death of their husbands, either through affection, or for the sake of the honour and reputation of their fathers and relations; but a thing like this was never known to be done by any mother, whether among the Muhammadans or Hindús.

On the 15th of the same month I bestowed the finest of my horses on Rájá Mán Singh in consequence of the affection which I entertained for him. As I had asked Jagat Singh, the eldest son of Rájá Mán Singh, for the hand of his daughter, I sent to the Rájá, on the 16th, a sum of 80,000 rupees on account of one of the nuptial ceremonies, called *sáchak*.[2] Mukarrab Khán sent me from the Port of Kambháit (Kambáy) a piece of European tapestry, which was so beautifully made that I had never seen any work of the Faringis equal to it before.

On the 4th of Rabí'u-l awwal, the daughter of Jagat Sing entered my Seraglio, and the nuptial ceremonies were performed in the residence of Mariam-i Zamán. Among other valuables which Rájá Mán Singh sent with her were sixty elephants.

As I was very anxious to extirpate the Ráná, I determined

---

[1] توبغن is said in the Turkí Dictionary to mean exclusively a white hawk. It is not found in Richardson's Dictionary.

[2] [Presentation of *Hinna* to the bride.]

to send Mahábat Khán against him, and placed 12,000 horse, perfectly equipped, with some experienced officers, under his command, besides 500 Ahadís, 2000 musketeers, artillery to the number of seventy or eighty guns, and elephant and camel-swivels, and sixty elephants. I also ordered a treasure of twenty *lacs* of rupees to be sent with this army.

Khán-khánán, who was my preceptor, came from Burhánpúr, and paid me a visit. He was so anxious to see me, that he did not know whether he came on foot or head. He threw himself in great agitation at my feet. With great kindness and favour I raised up his head with my hands, and with much affection took him in my arms and kissed his face. He presented me with two rosaries of rubies and pearls, and several rubies and emeralds, to the value of three *lacs* of rupees, besides many other articles of all sorts. * * *

On the 22nd Ásaf Khán presented me with a ruby seven *tánks* in weight, which was purchased by his brother Abú-l Kásim in the port of Kambháit for 75,000 rupees. Its colour and form were exceedingly good, but in my opinion it was not worth more than 60,000 rupees.

On the 24th the sons of Khán-khánán, who were coming after him, also arrived and paid their respects. They presented me with 25,000 rupees. On the same day the Khán also presented me with ninety elephants. This day a doe was brought, which freely allowed itself to be milked, and produced four *sers* of milk every day. Such a doe I had never seen or heard of. There is no difference of taste between the milk of a doe and that of a cow or a female buffalo. It is said to be a remedy for asthma.

On the 11th Rájá Mán Singh, in order to make his preparations for the equipment of the army of the Dakhin, whither he was ordered to proceed, asked for leave to go to Amber, his native country. I granted his request, and gave him an elephant, which was called Hushiyár Mast.

On the 21st Khán-khánán, having undertaken to suppress all

the disturbances which had arisen in the territory of Nizámu-l Mulk at the death of the late Emperor, wrote a document, in which he engaged that if he did not successfully perform this service within two years, he would confess himself liable to punishment, provided only that, besides the army which was already in the province, a force of 12,000 horse and a treasure of ten *lacs* of rupees be placed at his disposal. I ordered that he should immediately be provided with every equipment for the army, and gave him leave to proceed to his duty.

As Kishen Singh, the youngest maternal uncle of Khurram, had rendered many valuable services while with Mahábat Khán, and in the engagement with the army of the Ráná had received a spear-wound in his foot, had killed twenty of the Ráná's distinguished officers, and captured about 3000 men, he was now raised to the rank of 2000 personal salary, and the command of 1000 horse. * * *

On Tuesday the 17th, I went on foot to see the resplendent sepulchre of my father. If I could, I would travel this distance upon my eye-lashes or my head. My father, when he made a vow respecting my birth, had gone on foot from Fathpúr to Ajmír on a pilgrimage to the shrine of the great Khwájá Mu'ínu-d dín Chishtí, a space of 120 *kos*, and it would therefore be nothing very great if I were to go this short distance upon my head or eyes. When I had obtained the good fortune of visiting the tomb, and had examined the building which was erected over it, I did not find it to my liking. My intention was, that it should be so exquisite that the travellers of the world could not say they had seen one like it in any part of the inhabited earth. While the work was in progress, in consequence of the rebellious conduct of the unfortunate Khusrú, I was obliged to march towards Lahore. The builders had built it according to their own taste, and had altered the original design at their discretion. The whole money had been thus expended, and the work had occupied three or four years. I ordered that clever architects, acting in concert with some intelligent persons, should

pull down the objectionable parts which I pointed out. By
degrees a very large and magnificent building was raised, with
a nice garden round it, entered by a lofty gate, consisting of
minarets made of white stone. The total expense of this large
building was reported to me to amount to 50,000 *túmáns* of
'Irák, and forty-five *lacs* of *khánis* of Túrán.

On Sunday, the 23rd, I went to the house of Hakím 'Alí, to
see the reservoir, like one which was made in the time of my
father in Lahore. I was accompanied by a body of attendants
who had not seen it. The size of the reservoir was six yards
each way, and by its side was made a chamber, which was exceedingly well lighted, and which had a passage to it through the
water, but not a drop could penetrate the chamber. It was so
large that ten or twelve persons could sit in it. The Hakím presented me there with what money and articles he could produce
at the time. After seeing the chamber, and allowing all my
attendants to examine it, I returned to my palace, having
honoured the Hakím with the rank of 2000. * *

On the 6th of Zí-l hijja, Mukarrib Khán sent me a picture,
stating that the Portuguese believed it to be the portrait of
Tímúr. It was represented that, at the time when Ilderim
Báyazíd was taken prisoner by the victorious army of that
Emperor, a Christian, who was then the governor of Istambol,
sent an ambassador with presents to offer terms of submission.
He was accompanied by a painter, who drew a portrait of the
Emperor, and on his return carried it away with him. If this
had been true, in my opinion there could not have been a more
valuable curiosity in my possession; but as it bore no resemblance
to his royal descendants, I was not at all satisfied of the truth
of the statement.

FOURTH YEAR OF THE REIGN.

[The Nauroz of the Fourth Year fell on the 14th Zí-l hijja,
1017 (11th March, 1609).

It had now become manifest that, to secure the settlement of the Dakhin, one of the Princes must be sent thither, and I accordingly resolved upon sending Parwez.[1]]

FIFTH YEAR OF THE REIGN.

[The Nau-roz of the Fifth Year fell on the 24th Zí-l hijja, 1018 (10th March, 1610).]

Outbreak at Patna.

[On the 19th of Urdíbihisht, in the fifth year of my reign, a wonderful event took place in Patna, which is the chief residence of the governor of the province of Bihár. When Afzal Khán, the governor of the province, was about to march to Gorakpúr, which had been recently conferred on him in *jágír*, and which lies at about sixty *kos* distance from Patna, he placed the fort and the city in charge of Shaikh Banárasí and Ghiyás Zain Khání the *díwán*, and other *mansabdars*; but thinking that there was no enemy in the country, he never thought of making provision for the security of the fort and city.

It happened that in his absence a turbulent and seditious person of Uch, by name Kutb, came in the habit of a *fakír*, into the territory of Ujjainiya, which lies near Patna, and having made friends with some people of notorious character, declared himself to be Khusrú, and said that, having escaped from prison, he had come there; and that those who joined and helped him should share in his success. With such false words, he assured those foolish people of the truth of his pretensions. As his eyes had been branded in days gone by, he told those people that while he was in prison hot cups had been tied over his eyes, which had left that mark.[2] By these means he succeeded in collecting a number of horse and foot. As these insurgents had received intelligence of Afzal Khán's absence from Patna, they took advantage of the opportunity, and having entered the city,

---

[1] [Ásaf Khán was sent with him as his *atálik* or tutor.—*Ikbál-náma, Ma-ásir-i Jahángírí.*]

[2] [An attempt had been made to blind Khusrú. See *infrá*, Extract from *Intikháb-i Jahángír-Sháhí.*]

made an attack upon the fort. On one occasion Shaikh Banárasí, who was in the fort, being confounded, came down to the gate; but the enemy pushed in, and would not let him close it. Then he went with Ghiyás, and getting out of a window on the river-side, they procured a boat, and endeavoured to make their way to Afzal Khán.

The rebels, flushed with success, entered the fort, took posses-sion of all the property of Afzal Khán, and all the royal treasure. A number of the vagabonds and adventurers of the city and suburbs also joined with them. The intelligence of this outrage reached Afzal Khán in Gorakpúr, and Shaikh Banárasí and Ghiyás also arrived by water. Several letters from the city stated that the pretender was only an impostor, and had falsely assumed the name of Khusrú. Afzal Khán, depending upon the favour of God and the aid of my fortunate star, immediately marched against the insurgents. In five days he arrived at Patna. The enemy having left one of their leaders in the fort, marched out both horse and foot to oppose him, and took post at four *kos* from the city, on the river Punpun, in array of battle. The engagement began, and the insurgents, after a slight resist-ance, took to flight in consternation. A number of them fled back into the fort, but Afzal Khán pursued them so closely, that he prevented them from shutting the gate. In panic they rushed into the house of Afzal Khán, and there held out till the evening. They shot about thirty men with their arrows. The impostor at last, when his companions were going to hell, and he had become helpless, came out to the presence of Afzal Khán. The Khán, to quash the rebellion, put him to death on the same day, and sent several of his followers who had been captured into confinement. When I was informed of this outbreak, I had Shaikh Banárasí, Ghiyás Ríhání, and the other officers brought to Ágra. I then ordered that their heads and beards should be shaved, and that they should be dressed in sordid garments, and be paraded round the city on the backs of asses, as a punishment to them and as a warning to others.]

Affairs of the Dakhin.

[On the 2nd A'bán, Khán-khánán came to present himself before me. I had received many complaints, true or untrue, about him, so I was estranged from him, and did not treat him with that kindness and attention which I had ever shown him, and which I had seen my venerable father show him. He had been sent on service to the Dakhin for a certain time, in attendance upon Prince Parwez. He and other *amirs* had started on this important duty; but when he arrived at Burhánpúr, regardless of the time being unfavourable for operations, and the want of supplies and necessaries, he led Sultán Parwez and the army to the Bálághát. Ill-feeling and discord prevailed among the *amirs*, and at length the grain was exhausted, and none was to be obtained for money. The men were reduced to distress, and there was no means of carrying the matter further. Horses, camels, and other quadrupeds sank exhausted. So he patched up a sort of peace with the enemy, and conducted Sultán Parwez and the army back to Burhánpúr. This reverse and distress brought me many letters of complaint against Khán-khánán, but I did not believe all that was stated. A letter also came from Khán Jahán, in which he said, "All the disasters have happened through the bad management of the Khán-khánán. Either confirm him in his command, or recall him to Court and appoint me to perform the service. If 30,000 horse are sent as a reinforcement, I will undertake in the course of two years to recover all the Imperial territory from the enemy, to take Kandahár and other fortresses on the frontier, and to make Bíjápúr a part of the Imperial dominions. If I do not accomplish this in the period named, I will never show my face at Court again." As the relations between Khán-khánán and the other *sardars* were unsatisfactory, I did not think it right to uphold him, so I removed him, and appointed Khán Jahán to the command. * *

From the time of the conquest of Ahmadnagar by my late brother Dániyál to the present, the place had been under the command of Khwájá Beg Mirzá Safawi, a relation of Sháh

Tahmasp of Persia; but since their late successes, the Dakhinís had invested the town. Every effort was made to defend the place, and Khán-khánán, and the other *amirs* who were with Prince Parwez at Burhánpúr, marched' forth to relieve it. Through the jealousies and dissensions of the leaders, and from want of supplies, the army was conducted by improper roads through mountains and difficult passes, and in a short time it was disorganized, and so much in want of food, that it was compelled to retreat. The hopes of the garrison were fixed on this force, and its retreat filled them with despair. They desired to evacuate the place. Khwájá Beg Mirzá did his best to console and encourage them; but in vain, so he capitulated on terms, and retired with his men to Burhánpur. When the despatches arrived, and I found that the Khwájá had fought bravely and done his best, I promoted him to a *mansab* of 5000; and gave him a suitable *jágir*.]

SIXTH YEAR OF THE REIGN.

[New Year's Day of the sixth year fell on the 6th Muharram, 1020 (12th March, 1611).] * * *

One of the royal slaves, who was employed as an ornamental carver, presented me with a most extraordinary instance of his ingenuity. It was such a marvel as I had neither seen nor heard of before, and therefore a brief description of it will be interest-.ing. He had fixed within the shell of a filbert a piece of painted ivory, which he had divided into four compartments. The first contains five individuals. Two are wrestling with each other, the third stands with a spear, the fourth bears a heavy stone, and the fifth is sitting with his hands on the ground, with a staff, a bow, and a .cup before him. The second part represents a throne, on which a king sits under a magnificent canopy. One leg is crossed over the other, and he has a cushion behind his back. Five servants are in attendance round about him, and the shade of a tree spreads over the whole. The third part exhibits a party of rope-dancers. There is a long bamboo supported by three ropes. One man 'dances upon the rope in an extraordinary attitude. He holds his right leg at the back of his head by his left hand. There is a goat also standing on the top of a stick. The second man beats a drum which hangs round his neck, while the third person stands holding up his hands and looking at the rope. Five individuals are also standing by him, one bearing a stick in his hand. The fourth part represents a large tree, under which Jesus Christ is sitting. One man is bowing his head at the feet of Jesus, while an old man is talking with him. Four other men are standing by his side. In acknowledgment of this wonderful piece of workmanship, I rewarded the artist with a handsome present and an increase of his allowances. * * *

Regulations.

It had repeatedly come to my hearing, that the *amirs* at the frontier posts were in the habit of requiring certain observances to which they had no right, paying no regard to the established rules and ordinances. Accordingly, the *bakhshis* were ordered to issue *farmáns* prohibiting them from observing in future those practices which are peculiar to emperors. 1. Not to sit at the *jharoka* or window.[1] 2. Not to give the *amirs* and *sardárs* serving under them the annoyance of their own chair or of requiring obeisance to the chair.[2] 3. Not to have elephant fights. 4. Not to punish any person by ordering him to be blinded, or to have his nose or ears cut off. 5. Not to forcibly impose Musulmán burdens (*taklif-i Musulmáni*) on any one.[3] 6. Not to grant titles to their

---

[1] [Not to show themselves at the window to he people, as was the practice of emperors.]

[2] [The words are بامرا و سرداران كومكي تكليف چوكي خود و تسليم چوكي نكنند . The *Ma-ásir* repeats the exact words. The *Ikbál-náma* substitutes بندهاي پادشاهي (servants of the State) for the first part of the sentence, and leaves out the second *chauki* (chair). The meaning is perhaps this: "They were not to sit in state themselves nor to require obeisance to an empty chair placed for the Emperor."].

[3] [This prohibition is not repeated either in the *Ikbál-náma* or *Ma-ásir-i Jahángírí*.]

servants. 7. Not to require the servants of the State to bow their bodies or to touch the ground before them.[1] 8. Not to trouble the singers and musicians to give chairs after the manner of a *darbar*.[2] 9. Not to have the drums beaten at the time of their going out. 10. When they presented a horse or elephant to any man, whether a public or private servant, they were not to require obeisance from him with a horse's bridle or an elephant's goad placed upon his back. 11. Not to make the royal servants to walk on foot in their retinue. 12. Not to place their seals upon letters addressed to royal servants. These rules, which were promulgated under the title of *A'in-i Jahangiri*, are now in force.

SEVENTH YEAR OF THE REIGN.

[New Year's Day of the seventh year fell on the 17th Muharram, 1021 (12th March, 1612).]

War in Bengal.

[Just at this time, a despatch arrived from Islám Khán, with intelligence of the defeat of the enemy, and the deliverance of the country of Bengal from the sway of 'Usmán the Afghán. Before entering upon this subject, a few particulars respecting Bengal may be recorded. It is an extensive country, situated in the second clime. Its length is 450 *kos*, extending from Bandar Chátgám (the port of Chittagong) to Garhí, and its breadth, from the northern mountains to the province of Madáran (Midnapúr), is 220 *kos*. Its revenue amounted to sixty *krors* of *dáms*.[3] In former times, its governors always maintained 8000 horse, one *lac* of foot soldiers, 1000 elephants, and 400 or 500 war boats. From the time of Sher Khán Afghán and his son Salím Khán,

---

[1] [To make *kornish* or *taslim*.]

[2] [تكليف چوكي دادن نكنند] The *Ikbál-náma* omits this interdict. The *Ma-ásir* transposes the words "*chauki dádan*" and reads "*dádan-i chauki*." There would seem to be some conventional meaning of the words "*taklif chauki*," which was not generally understood even when these works were written.]

[3] [One *kror* and fifty *lacs* of rupees.—*Ikbál-náma*.]

this country had remained in the possession of the Afgháns.[1] When my revered father mounted and adorned the throne of Hindústán, he appointed an army to subdue it. Strenuous efforts to effect its conquest were for a long time maintained, and at length it was wrested from the hands of Dáúd Kiráni, the last ruler of the country, who was killed, and his forces defeated and scattered by Khán Jahán.

From that time to the present the country has been governed by servants of the Empire, excepting only a remnant of Afgháns who remained in the recesses and on the borders of the country. By degrees these fell into trouble and distress, and the whole country was annexed to the Imperial dominions. When I ascended the throne, in the first year of my reign, I recalled Mán Singh, who had long been governor of the country, and appointed my *kokaltásh* Kutbu-d dín to succeed him. Soon after his arrival, he was assassinated by one of the turbulent characters of the country, who met with his reward and was killed.[2] Jahángír Kulí Khán, whom I had made a commander of 5000, was governor of the province of Bihár, and was near to Bengal, so I ordered him to proceed thither and take possession of the country. Islám Khán was then at Ágra, and I sent a *farmán* to him, granting him the province of Bihár in *jágír*, and directing him to proceed there. Jahángír Kulí Khán had not been long there when he fell ill, and died from the effects of the climate. On receiving intelligence of his death, I appointed Islám Khán to succeed him, and sent directions for him to proceed thither with all speed, leaving Bihár in charge of Afzal Khán.

On my appointing him to this great service, some of my servants made remarks upon his youth and want of experience, but I perceived that he had nobility of character and talents, so I selected him. The result has been, that he has brought the

---

[1] ["After the death of Salím Khán, Sulaimán Kiráni ruled over it."—*Ikbál-náma*.]

[2] [Sher-Afgán, first husband of Núr Jahán.—See post, Extracts from the *Ikbál-náma*.]

country into a state of order, such as no one of his predecessors
in the office had ever been able to accomplish. One of his most
signal services has been the suppression of 'Usmán the Afghán.
During the reign of my father, the royal forces had continual
encounters with this man, but were unable to subdue him

Islám Khán took up his quarters at Dacca, to bring the *zamíndárs* of that vicinity to submission, and he formed the design of
sending an army against 'Usmán and his country, to induce him
to make profession of allegiance, or else to exterminate him and
his turbulent followers. Shujá'at Khán was at this time with
Islám Khán, and he was appointed to command the force appointed for this service. Several other of the servants of the
State, such as * *, were sent with him. * * When they arrived
near 'Usmán's fortress and country, some able speakers were sent
to advise him to renounce his rebellious habits, and to become a
good subject; but he was too proud and ambitious. He cherished
the design of subduing this country, and had other projects in
his head. He would not listen to a word, but got ready for
battle. He took a position in a village on the bank of a *nála*,
surrounded by water and marsh. Shujá'at Khán determined
to attack, and arranged his forces in their respective places.
'Usmán had not intended to fight that day; but when he heard
that the Imperial forces were in motion, he mounted and rode to
the bank of the *nála* to arrange his men.

The battle began, and the fight waxed warm. At the very
first the bold rebel, mounted on a fierce elephant, pushed forward
and encountered the advanced force. After a sharp struggle, the
commanders of the attacking force were killed. Iftikhár Khán,
the commander of the right wing, showed no want of gallantry,
and was killed fighting, while his men fought desperately till
they were cut to pieces. In the left wing also Kishwar Khán
fell, after performing great deeds of valour.

Although the enemy had lost many men, their intrepid leader
conceived a well-devised and skilful movement.[1] He knew that

[1]. [He was very fat and heavy, and rode on an elephant in a *howda.—Ikbál-náma.*]

the commanders of the advance and of the right and left wings had fallen, but that the centre remained. So, heedless of his dead and wounded, he made a fierce assault upon the centre. The sons and brothers and relatives of Shujá'at Khán, with some others, cast themselves in his way like lions and panthers, and fought desperately tooth and nail, till many of them were slain, and such as survived were severely wounded.

The leading elephant, a very fierce one, attacked Shujá'at Khán, and he wounded it with his spear, but what does such an animal care for a spear? Shujá'at drew his sword and gave it two cuts, but what did it care for that? He then wounded it twice with his dagger, but even then it did not turn, but sought to bear down both the Khán and his horse. As he was thrown from his horse, he shouted "Jahángír Sháh!" and then sprung to his feet. One of his attendants struck the elephant on his fore-legs with a two-handed sword, and brought him to his knees. Shujá'at and his attendant then threw his driver to the ground, and with the same dagger he wounded the elephant in the trunk and forehead so that he shrieked with pain and turned back. The animal had received so many wounds, that he fell on reaching the enemy's ranks.

Shujá'at Khán's horse got up unhurt; but while he was mounting, the baffled foe drove another elephant against the standard-bearer of Shujá'at Khán, to overthrow both horse and standard. Shujá'at raised a shout of warning to the standard-bearer, and cried, "Act like a man, I am yet alive." Every man near the standard directed his arrow, his dagger, or his sword against the elephant. Shujá'at Khán bade the standard-bearer arise, and calling for another horse, made him remount and again raise the standard.

During this struggle, a musket-ball struck the forehead of the rebel commander, but the hand which fired it was never known, though inquiry was made. As soon as he received the wound, 'Usmán fell back, for he knew that it was mortal. Still for two watches and a half, in spite of his wound, he kept urging his men on, and the fight and slaughter was continued. At length the foe gave way, and the troops pursued them to the position they had fortified. Still they kept up a discharge of arrows and muskets, and prevented the royal forces from obtaining an entrance.

When Walí the brother, and Mamrez the son, of 'Usmán, and other of his friends, were informed of the severe wound he had received, they knew that he could not survive; they also reflected that if after such a defeat they broke and made for their fastnesses, not one of them would escape; so they resolved to remain in their position for the night, and to escape just before break of day to their fortresses. At midnight 'Usmán departed to hell. and in the following watch the enemy, carrying off his body, and leaving all their equipage standing, made off to their strongholds. Upon hearing of their flight, Shujá'at Khán proposed to pursue them, and not give them time to draw breath; but the exhaustion of the troops, the burying of the dead, and the tending of the wounded, prevented him, to his great chagrin. 'Abdu-l Islám, son of Mu'azzam Khán, now arrived with several officers, 600 horse, and 400 gunners. With these fresh troops he started in pursuit. Walí, who was now the leader of the rebels, on being informed of this, (*resolved to ask for peace*). Shujá'at Khán and the other officers accepted the proposition, and granted terms. Next day Walí, and the sons and relations of 'Usmán, came into the Imperial camp, and presented forty-nine elephants, with other tribute. Shujá'at Khán then left some forces to watch the country held by the enemy, while he carried Walí and his Afghán prisoners to Jahángír-nagar (Dacca), which he entered on the 6th Safar, and waited on Islám Khán. * * In reward of this service, I raised Islám Khán to the dignity of 6000, and I gave Shujá'at Khán the title of " Rustam of the age," with a *mansab* of 1000.] * * *

On the 16th of the month of Farwardín, Mukarrab Khán, one of my chief, confidential and oldest nobles, having received

the dignity of 3000, and the command of 2000 horse, gained the
honour of being presented to me on his arrival from Kambay.
Certain political considerations induced me to depute him to the
seaport town of Goa,[1] to visit the *wazir* or ruler of that place.
I further asked him to purchase certain articles procurable there,
which might suit my taste. In obedience to orders, he set out
directly for that harbour, and resided there for a long time. He
did not regard the expense, but purchased several articles from
the Feringís, at any price they asked. On his return, he presented
the precious things he had bought in Goa. Amongst these were
a few animals which excited my curiosity, and which I had never
seen before. No one even knew their names.

The Emperor Bábar has in his Memoirs given an able description and pictured representation of several animals; but it is
most probable he never ordered the painters to draw them from
the life. But as the animals now before me were of such exquisite
rarity, I wrote a description of them, and order I that their
pictures should be drawn in the *Jahángír-náma*, with the view
that their actual likenesses might afford a greater surprise to the
reader than the mere description of them. One of the birds
resembled a peahen, but was a little larger in size, though less than
a peacock. When he was desirous of pairing, he used to spread
his tail and feathers, and danced about like a peacock. His beak
and feet resembled those of a barn-door fowl. His head, neck,
and throat changed their colour every minute; but when anxious
to pair, he became a perfect red, and seemed to be a beautiful
piece of coral. After some time, he was as white as cotton, and
sometimes he got as blue as a turquoise, and in short turned all
colours like a chameleon. The piece of flesh which is attached
to his head looked like the comb of a cock. But the curious
part of it was this, that piece of flesh, when he was about to pair,

---

[1] Though this is spelt Goa, or rather Goh, in the original, it is most probable that
Goga is meant; and indeed in one copy it is spelt Goda, where the *d* may have been
inserted for *g*. Goa was much beyond Mukarrab Khán's jurisdiction; whereas Goga
was in it. Goga is the seaport of Ahmadábád, and was at one time the chief port of
the Gulf of Kambay.—See Briggs's *Cities of Gujarishtan*, p. 281.

hung down a span long, like the trunk of an elephant, and when
again restored to its position, it was erected over his head to the
height of two fingers, like the horn of a rhinoceros. The part
round his eyes remained constantly of a blue colour, and was
never subject to change, which was not the case with his wings,
which were always changing their colour, contrary to those of a
peacock.[1] * * *

I put the *tiká* on the forehead of Dalpat with my Royal
hands, selected him as the successor of his father, and conferred
upon him the *jágír* and country of the deceased Rái Singh. A
handsome ornamented inkstand and pen was this day given by
I'timádu-d daula.

Lakhmí Chand, the Rájá of Kamáun, one of the chief Rájás
in the hills, was son of Rájá Rái, who, at the time of waiting upon
the late King, sent a petition, asking that the son of Rájá Todar
Mal might lead him to the royal presence, and his request was
complied with. Lakhmí Chand now likewise begged me to order
the son of I'timádu-d daula to conduct him to the Court; and to
meet his wishes, I sent Sháhpúr to bring him into my presence.
The hill-chief had brought a great number of the valuable rarities
of his mountains for my acceptance. Amongst them were beautiful strong ponies called *Gúts*, several hawks and falcons,
numerous pods of musk, and whole skins of the musk-deer
with the musk in them. He also presented me with various
swords which were called *khandah* and *katára*. This Rájá
is the richest hill-chief, and it is said that there is a gold mine
in his territory.

As Khwája Jahán had greatly distinguished himself in architecture, I sent him to Lahore to build a handsome palace for me.

Defeat in the Dakhin.

[Affairs in the Dakhin were in a very unsatisfactory state, in
consequence of the bad generalship and want of care of Khán-i

---

[1] This description is evidently meant for a turkey-cock—which, strange to say, is
in Turkish ascribed to India, and called *Hind Táüghi*.—See David's *Turkish Grammar*,
p. 133.

'azam, and a defeat had been suffered by 'Abdu-lla Khán. I summoned Khwája Abú-l Hasan to my presence, and after inquiry, I ascertained that the disaster was attributable partly to the conceit and rashness of 'Abdu-lla Khán, and partly to discord and want of co-operation among the *amirs*.

'Abdu-lla Khán and the officers who had been appointed to serve under him, marched with the army of Gujarát by way of Násik Tirbang. This force was well equipped; its numbers were from 10,000 to 14,000, and the officers serving in it were * *. It had been arranged that another force should advance from the side of Birár under the command of Rájá Mán Singh, Khán-Jahán, the *Amíru-l Umará*, and other officers. These two armies were to keep up communications, and to be informed of each other's movements, so that they might at an appointed time close in upon the enemy. If this plan had been carried out frankly and cordially without jealousy, it is very probable that under God's grace it would have succeeded.

'Abdu-lla Khán, having passed the Gháts, entered the country of the enemy, but made no arrangements for sending messengers to obtain intelligence of the other force, and to regulate his movements in concert, so as to place the enemy between the two armies. He trusted entirely to his own power, and thought that if he could effect the victory himself, it would be all the better. Acting upon this view, he paid no heed to Rájá Mán Singh when the latter wished to settle a concerted plan.

The enemy kept a sharp watch over his movements, and sent a large force of Mahrattas (*bargiyán*), who skirmished with him all day, and harassed him at night with rockets and other fiery projectiles, till the main body of the enemy drew near, and he was quite unaware of their proximity, although he approached Daulat-ábád, a stronghold of the Dakhinís. * * 'Ambar the black-faced, who had placed himself in command of the enemy, continually brought up reinforcements till he had assembled a large force, and he constantly annoyed 'Abdu-lla with rockets and various kinds of fiery missiles (*átash-bázi*), till he reduced him to a sad

condition. So, as the Imperial army had received no reinforcements, and the enemy was in great force, it was deemed expedient
to retreat, and prepare for a new campaign. All the chiefs were
unanimous in favour of this, and before dawn they began to fall
back. The enemy pressed upon them to the boundaries of their
own territory, but either side held its own. But a party of our
force courted a serious encounter, and 'Alí Mardán Khán, after a
valorous conflict, was left wounded in the hands of the enemy.[1] * *
After another day, when they reached the frontier of Rájá
Baharjíú, an adherent of the Imperial throne, the enemy retired,
and 'Abdu-lla Khán proceeded to Gujarát. It seems clear, that if
proper precautions had been taken, and the two forces had been
kept in co-operation, the objects of the campaign would have been
accomplished. On the retreat of 'Abdu-lla, the army, which
marched by way of Birár, had no alternative but to retire ; so
it retreated and joined the camp of Prince Parwez, near Burhánpúr. On receiving this information, I was greatly excited, and
felt inclined to proceed thither myself to retrieve the position.
But Khwája Abú-l Hasan remonstrated * *, and I resolved to
send Khán-khánán * *.

The Dakhinís now made proposals for peace. 'Ádil Khán pro-
fessed amity, and promise[1], if the affairs of the Dakhinís
were left to him, that he would restore sundry districts to the
Imperial officers. I did not come to any decision on the matter,
but left it to Khán-khánán.]

EIGHTH YEAR OF THE REIGN.

[The eighth New Year's Day of my reign fell on the 26th
Muharram, 1022 A.H. (8th March, 1613 A.D.).]

Journey to Ajmir and Campaign against the ' .á.

[On the 2nd Sha'bán I left Ágra, with the intention of paying

---

[1] [He was carried to Daulatábád, and Malik 'Ambar appointed a surgeon to attend
him, but he died in a few days. A saying of his, continues the *Ikbál-náma*, has
become famous. A person attending him observed, "Victory is in the hands of
heaven." He replied, " Truly victory is with heaven, but the battle is for man."]

a visit to Ajmír, having two objects in view. One, to pay a visit
to the tomb of Khwája Mu'ínu-d dín Chishtí, whose blessed
influence had operated so powerfully on the fortunes of my
dynasty. Second, to overcome and subjugate Amar Singh, who
was the greatest of the *zamíndárs* and *rájás* of Hindústán. All
the *rájás* and *ráis* of the country have acknowledged him and
his ancestors to be their chief and head. The sovereignty and
government have been held by this family for a long time. For
many years they held rule in the east country, and then had the
title of *Rájá*. Afterwards they fell upon the Dakhin, and brought
the greater part of that country under their sway, when they
took the title of *Rúp*, " handsome," instead of that of *Rájá*. After
that they overran the mountain land of Mewat, and still advanc-
ing they got possession of the fortress of Jaipúr.

From that date [1] up to the present year, which is the eighth of
my reign, 1471 years have passed. Twenty-six individuals of
this race have reigned over a period amounting to 1010 years,
who have borne the title of *Ráwal*. From the time of Rahab,
who was the first to assume the title of Ráná, to Ráná Amar
Singh, who is the present Ráná, there have been twenty-six
persons, who have reigned over a period of 461 years. During all
this long period not one of them had bowed the neck in submission to any King or Emperor of Hind. They were nearly
always in a state of insubordination and rebellion. So, in the
days of the Emperor Bábar, the Ráná Sángá, having assembled
all the *Rájás* and *Ráis* of this country, with 180,000 horsemen
and several hundred thousand infantry, fought a battle in the
vicinity of Bayána against the victorious army of the Musulmáns,
and suffered a signal defeat. The full particulars of this battle
are given in that most trustworthy work, the *Wáki'át*, written
by the Emperor Bábar himself. My father also devoted himself
with great ardour to the subjection of this unruly race. Several
times he sent expeditions against them, and in the twelfth year of

---

[1] [It does not distinctly appear what " that date " means. Inferentially it would
seem to signify the time when the title " *Rúp* " was used.]

his reign he marched in person to effect the reduction of Chítor, one of the strongest fortresses in the world, and to subdue the country of the Ráná. After a siege of four months and ten days, he overpowered the men of Amar Singh's father, took the fortress, and then returned. Repeatedly he sent armies against the Ráná, and each time they pressed him so hardly that he was reduced to the brink of ruin, when something occurred to save him from destruction. Near the end of his reign, my father, having directed his own attention to the conquest of the Dakhin, sent me with a large army and trusty leaders against the Ráná. For reasons too lengthy to be here entered upon, both these enterprises failed.

When the Empire devolved upon me, as this conquest had been half effected under my leading, the first army I sent upon foreign service after my accession was this army against the Ráná. My son Parwez was appointed to command, and all the resources of my government were applied to the service. Ample treasure and abundant artillery were ready to be sent off, when all was stopped by the unhappy outbreak of Khusrú. I was obliged to pursue him to the Panjáb, and the capital and interior of the country were denuded of troops. I was obliged to write to Parwez, directing him to return to protect Ágra and the neighbourhood, and to remain there; so the campaign against the Ráná was suspended. When, by the favour of God, I had quashed Khusrú's rebellion, I returned to Ágra, and I then sent Mahábat Khán, 'Abdu-lla Khán, and other *amírs* against the Ráná; but until I started from Ajmír, the Imperial forces had not achieved any success of importance. There was nothing to detain me in Ágra, and I felt assured that nothing of any importance would be accomplished till I myself went thither.

At the time appointed, I left Ágra and encamped in the garden of Dahra. The next day was the festival of the *Dasahra*, and according to rule the horses and elephants were decked out and paraded before me. The mothers [1] (*wálidahá*) and sisters of

---

[1] It has already been recorded (page 294) that Khusrú's mother had poisoned herself.

Khusrú represented that he was exceedingly contrite and sorry for what he had done. Having thus excited my paternal affection, I called him into my presence, and arranged that he should come every day to pay his respects to me. I stayed in the garden twenty days, and on the 21st day of Mihr I started, having appointed Khwája Jahán to the charge of the capital, with its palaces and treasures. On the 2nd Mihr, intelligence arrived that Rájá Bású had died at Sháhábád, on the Ráná's frontier. On the 10th I encamped at Rúp-bás, now called Amánábád. It was formerly the *jágír* of Rúp, but after him I gave it to Amánu-lla son of Mahábat Khán, and I ordered that it should be called by his name. It was one of my regular hunting-grounds, so I went out hunting every day. In these few days 158 deer, male and female, and other kinds of game were killed. * * On the 10th Ramazán intelligence arrived of the death of Kalíj Khán, one of the oldest servants of the State, in his eightieth year. He was engaged at Peshawar in controlling the Afgháns.] * * *

In this month (A'zur) news arrived that the Europeans in Goa, in defiance of their engagements, had plundered four ships engaged in the foreign trade of the port of Surat; and having made a great many Muhammadans prisoners, had at the same time taken possession of their money and goods. It gave me much displeasure. Mukarrab Khán, the governor of that harbour, received a dress of honour, besides an elephant and horse, and was commanded to proceed to put a stop to such outrages. He started on the 18th of A'zur. * * *

Campaign against the Ráná.

[After visiting the tomb of the saint Mu'ínu-d dín Chishtí, the matter of the Ráná was again taken into consideration, and I now determined to stay at Ajmír, and to send my dear son Khurram on the expedition. On the 6th I gave him leave to depart, and made him many presents.[1] Besides the men who had already been sent on this service under Khán-i 'azam, I now placed 12,000 horse under the command of the Prince, and after

---

[1] [The text specifies them.]

granting presents to the officers, I despatched them. Fidáí Khán was appointed *Bakhshí.* * * Although Khán-i 'azam had requested me to send Khurram on this service, and the Prince himself treated him with much attention, he did not show a proper spirit, and acted in an unsatisfactory matter. I wrote him a very kind letter, * * but my words had no effect upon him, and he still went on in a foolish obstinate way. When Khurram found that he was not hearty in the work, he wrote to me that it was by no means desirable to keep him there, and that his relations with Khusrú were the cause of his misbehaviour. So I ordered Mahábat Khán to go to Udípúr and bring him away, and I ordered Muhammad Takí Díwán to proceed to Mandisor and convey to Ajmír his children and dependents. * * On the 16th, I received a despatch from Khurram, informing me that an elephant of which the Ráná was very fond, and seventeen others, had been taken. He added that their master would soon be a prisoner.]

Ninth Year of the Reign.

[The New Year's Day of the ninth year of my reign fell on a day corresponding with the 9th Safar, 1023 H. (1614 A.D.).

Mahábat Khán, who had been sent to fetch Khán-i 'azam and his son 'Abdu-lla, arrived. I consigned Khán-i 'azam to Ásaf Khán, to custody at Gwálior, but to be honourably treated.

On the 18th Urdíbihist, I forbad Khusrú to come to my presence. In consequence of my paternal affection, and the supplications of his mothers and sisters, I had given orders that he should come to pay his respects to me every day. But he showed no signs of frankness of spirit, and always seemed sad and downcast, so I forbad his coming to see me.]

'Atr of Roses.

['*Atr* of roses, the most excellent of perfumes, was discovered in my reign. The mother of Núr Jahán Begam conceived the idea of collecting the oil which rises to the surface when rose-water is heated, and this having been done, the oil was found to be a most powerful perfume.]

Submission of the Ráná.

[In the month of Bahman, intelligence came in of the submission of Ráná Amar Singh, and of his willingness to pay homage to the Imperial throne. The particulars of the matter are these: My dear and fortunate son Sultán Khurram had established several military posts, especially in places where, from the insalubrity of the climate, the bad quality of the water, and the difficulty of access, many persons deemed it impossible to form a station. By this, and by keeping the Imperial forces in continual movement against the enemy, regardless of the intensity of the heat and the abundance of rain, he had captured the families of many Singhs, and had brought the enemy to such straits, that the Ráná perceived he could hold out only a little longer, and that he must either flee from his country or be made a prisoner. Being helpless, he resolved to succumb, and to do homage. He sent his maternal uncle Subh Káran, and Hardás Jhálá one of his most trusty and intelligent servants, praying my son to overlook his offences, and to give him an assurance of safety under the princely seal; he would then wait upon him in person to pay homage, and would send his son and heir-apparent to the Imperial Court, so that he might be classed among the adherents of the throne like all other *rájás*. He also begged that on account of old age he might be excused from proceeding to Court.

My son sent these persons to me in charge of Mullá Shukru-lla, his *díwán*, who, after the settlement of this matter, was dignified with the title of Afzal Khán, and of Sundar Dás, who afterwards received the title of Rái Ráyán. My son wrote me the particulars in a despatch. * * Ráná Amar Singh and his ancestors, relying upon the security of his mountains and his home, had never seen one of the kings of Hindústán, and had never shown obedience; but now in my fortunate reign he had been compelled to make his submission. In compliance with my son's letter, I overlooked the Ráná's offences, and wrote him a kind and re-assuring *farmán* under my own seal. I also wrote a kind letter to the Ráná's son, desiring him to specify the way in which he would come to pay his respects, and assuring him that all things should be made pleasant for him. My son sent my letters to the Ráná, to comfort him, and to gratify him with the expectation of my favour and kindness, and it was arranged that the Ráná and his sons should have an interview with my son on the 28th Bahman.]

Good News.

The second happy tidings was the death of Bahadúr, son of the chief of Gujarát, and the leaven of insubordination and turbulence. God of his mercy destroyed him, but he died a natural death.

The third happy tidings was the defeat of the Portuguese (*Warzi*), who had made every preparation for the capture of the port of Surat. An action took place between them and the English,[1] who had sought refuge in that port. Most of their vessels were burnt by the English, and not being able to stand the contest, they took to flight, and sent a message to Mukarrab Khán, the governor of the ports of Gujarát, suing for peace, and representing that they had come with peaceful views, not to fight, and that the English had been the first to quarrel.

[Another piece of intelligence that came was, that the Rájpúts who had resolved to kill (Malik) 'Ambar had concealed themselves till they found an opportunity of approaching him, when one of them gave him an ineffectual wound. The men in the escort of 'Ambar killed the Rájpút, and carried their master off home. A very little more would have made an end of this cursed fellow.]

[At the end of the month, while I was hunting in the environs of Ajmír, Muhammad Beg arrived with a letter from my son Sultán Khurram. * * From the letter it appeared that on the 26th Bahman the Ráná came in and paid his respects to my son, with all the observances required by the rules of the Imperial

---

[1] *Angrezán.* This is perhaps the first occasion of the use of that word in a native book.

Court. He presented as tribute a celebrated ruby belonging to his family, and * *. My son received him with great kindness; and when the Ráná advanced to kiss the Prince's feet, and beg pardon for his offences, the Prince raised him up, did his best to cheer him, and presented him with a jewelled sword, etc., etc. It is the practice among *zamíndárs*, that they, and the son who is heir-apparent, never present themselves before kings together; so the Ráná had not brought his son Karan, who was his heir. But the Prince wished to depart on that same day, so the Ráná took his leave, and sent his son Karan to wait upon Khurram, and on the same day he started with the Prince on his journey to the Imperial Court.]

Tenth Year of the Reign.

[The New Year's Day of my tenth year corresponded with the 8th[1] Safar, 1024 H. * *

Karan (son of the Ráná) was granted a *mansab* of 5000, and I gave him a small rosary of emeralds and pearls with a ruby in the middle, such as in Hindi is called *Smarani.* * *]

Drinking.

[The 25th of De was the day of the annual weighing of my son Khurram. He was now twenty-four years of age, a married man, and the father of a family, but yet he had never been addicted to drinking wine. This being the day for weighing him, I said to him, " My boy, you are the father of children, and kings and princes drink wine. To-day is a festival, and I will drink wine with you, and I give you leave to drink on feast days, on New Year's Day, and at great entertainments, but always with moderation; for to drink to excess and weaken the intellect is avoided by the wise; in fact, some good and benefit ought to be obtained from wine-drinking."

Up to my fourteenth year I had never drunk wine, except two or three times in childhood, when my mother or nurses had given me some as a remedy for some childish ailment. Once also my

---

[1] [This ought to be the 18th, corresponding to 10th March, 1615.]

father called for some spirit ('*arak*) to the amount of a *tola*, and mixing it with rose-water, made me drink it as a remedy for a cough. In the days when my father was in the field against the Yúsufzáí Afgháns, and was encamped near Atak, on the Níláb (Indus), I one day went out hunting. I met with many mishaps, and was very tired, when one of my attendants told me that if I would drink a cup of wine, it would relieve my fatigue and weariness. I was young, and prone to indulgence, so I sent a servant to the house of Hakím 'Alí for a refreshing drink. He brought me about a cup (*piyála*) and a half of yellow wine of sweet taste in a small bottle, and I drank it. The result was pleasant. From that time I took to wine-drinking, and from day to day took more and more, until wine of the grape had no effect upon me, and I resorted to spirit-drinking. In the course of nine years I got up to twenty cups of double-distilled spirit, fourteen of which I drank in the day, and the remaining six at night. The weight of this was six *sirs* of Hindústán, equal to one *man* of Írán. My food in those days was one fowl and some bread. No one dared to expostulate with me, and matters reached such an extreme, that when in liquor I could not hold my cup for shaking and trembling. I drank, but others held the cup for me. At last I sent for the *hakim* (doctor) Humám, brother of Hakím Abú-1 Fath, who was one of my father's attendants, and placed my case before him. With great kindness and interest, he spoke to me without concealment, and told me that if I went on drinking spirits in this way for six months longer, my state would be past remedy. His advice was good, and life is dear. I was greatly affected by his words, and from that day I began to diminish my potations, but I took to eating *falúhá*.[1] As I lessened my drink, I increased the *falúhá;* and I directed that my spirits should be mixed with wine of the grape; two parts wine and one spirit. Lessening my allowance daily, I reduced it in the course of seven years to six cups, each cup

---

[1] [This word is variously written *falúhá, falúhán, falúniyó, falúniyán.* It is, no doubt, the name of some intoxicating drug or preparation; perhaps *bháng.*]

weighing eighteen *miskáls* and a quarter. For fifteen years I have now kept to this quantity, taking neither more nor less. I take it at night, except on Thursday, that being the day of my accession to the throne, and on Friday, which is the most holy day in the week, for I do not think it right to pass these nights in heedlessness, and to fail in giving thanks to the Almighty for his blessings. On Thursday and on Sunday I eat no meat; that being the day of my accession, this my father's birthday. These days are held in great honour. After some time, instead of *falúhá,* I took to opium. Now that my age is forty-six years and four months solar reckoning, and forty-seven years nine months lunar style, I take eight *surkhs*[1] of opium when five hours of the day have passed, and six *surkhs* after one hour of the evening.]

Victories.

Towards the end of the year, tidings of victory arrived from all quarters of my dominions. The first victory was that won over Ahdád the Afghán, who had long been in rebellion in the mountains of Kábul. * *

Another victory was achieved over the army of the wretched 'Ambar. The following is a brief account of it. Some good officers and a body of *Bargis* (Mahrattas), a very hardy race of people, who are great movers of opposition and strife, being offended with 'Ambar, desired to become subjects to my throne. Having received assurances from Shahsawár Khán, who was with the royal army at Bálápúr, Ádam Khán, Yákút Khán, and other chiefs, with the *Bargis* Jádú Rái and Bábá Jukayath, came to see him, and he gave them each a horse, an elephant, a robe, and cash, according to their respective ranks. Having thus brought them into the interests of the throne, he marched with them from Bálápúr against 'Ambar. On their way they were opposed by an army of the Dakhinís; but they soon defeated it, and drove the men in panic to the camp of 'Ambar. In his

---

[1] [The *surkh* or *rati* is the seed of the *Abrus precatorius,* which averages about 1 $\frac{7}{8}$ of a grain Troy (Wilson). The old *rati* was 1·75 gr.; Akbar's coin *rati* ran as high as 1·90 (Thomas).]

vanity and pride, he resolved to hazard a battle with my victorious army. To his own forces he united the armies of 'Adil Khán and Kutbu-l Mulk, and with a train of artillery he marched to meet the royal army till he came within five or six *kos* of it.

On Sunday, the 25th of Bahman, they came to an engagement. At about three o'clock in the afternoon the fight commenced with rockets and guns, and at last Dáráb Khán, who commanded the foremost division, with other chiefs and warriors, drew their swords and vigorously attacked the enemy's advanced force. Their bravery and courage soon put their opponents to confusion. Without turning aside, they then fell upon the centre. In the same manner each division attacked the division which was before it, and the fight was terrible to behold. The battle went on for about an hour, and heaps of corpses were formed. 'Ambar, unable to withstand the royal army, fled from the field; and had it not been a very dark night, none of the enemy would have escaped. The great warriors of the royal army pursued the fugitives for about two or three *kos*, till horse and man were unable to move. The enemy was totally defeated and dispersed, and the warriors returned to their camp. All the enemy's guns, with 300 camels laden with rockets, many elephants, horses, and munitions of war to an incalculable extent, fell into the hands of the victorious army. The killed and wounded were innumerable, and a great number of chiefs were captured alive. Next day the army having moved from Fathpúr, marched towards Khirkí, which had been the shelter of the rebels ; but no trace of them was found. It encamped there, and learnt that the enemy were completely disorganized.

The third conquest achieved in those days was that by which the territory of Kokrah and its diamond mines were taken possession of, through the enterprising exertions of Ibráhím Khán. The territory belongs to the province of Bihár and Patna, and through it there runs a stream, from which diamonds are extracted in a very peculiar manner. In the days when the water is low, and is left in little holes and troughs, the people whose business it is to extract the diamonds, and who have great expertness in the art, search out for those portions from which they observe many little insects issue like gnats, which are called in the language of those people *chika*. These parts, along the whole course of the stream which is accessible, they fence round with a wall of stones, and then dig it up with spades and axes, to about one yard and a half deep, and search among the stones and mud which are brought up. In such soil both large and small diamonds are found, and sometimes so large that they are worth even a *lac* of rupees. In short, this territory and the stream from the bed of which diamonds are extracted were in the possession of Durjan Sál, *zamindár*. Although the governors of the province of Bihár had several times led their armies to invade his dominions, yet, on account of the impassable roads and thick forests, they were obliged to return, being contented only with two or three diamonds which he presented to them.

When the governorship of the province was transferred from Zafar Khán to Ibráhím Khán, I instructed the latter, on his departure to the province, to invade the dominion of that refractory chief, and dispossess him. Accordingly, Ibráhím, immediately after his arrival in the province, collected a force and marched against the *zamindár;* who, as on former occasions, sent him some diamonds and elephants; but the Khán did not accept them, and having proceeded with all speed, invaded his dominions. Before the enemy could collect his force, Ibráhím penetrated into his territory, and before the news of his approach could reach him, attacked the hill and the valley where he resided. Ibráhím ordered his people to search for him, and he was at last found in a valley with one of his brothers and some women, among whom was his mother and other wives of his father. All the diamonds which they had were taken, and twenty-three elephants fell into the hands of the royal army. As a reward for this service, the *mansab* of Ibráhím Khán was raised to the personal salary of 4000 and the command of 4000 horse, with the title of Fath-Jang. In like manner promotions

were ordered to be made in the rank of all those who had shown
distinguished bravery in the accomplishment of this undertaking.
The territory is still under the possession of the officers of this
government; and diamonds which are extracted from the stream
are brought to this Court. Recently, a diamond was found, the
value of which was estimated at the amount of 50,000 rupees,
and it is hoped that if the search be continued, more excellent
diamonds will be placed in the repository of the crown jewels.

Eleventh Year of the Reign.

The *Nau-roz* of the eleventh year of my reign corresponded
with the 1st Rabí'u-l awwal, 1025 h. (10th March, 1616 a.d.).

In this year, or rather in the tenth year of my reign, a dreadful
plague (*wabá*) broke out in many parts of Hindústán. It first
appeared in the districts of the Panjáb, and gradually came to
Lahore. It destroyed the lives of many Muhammadans and
Hindús. It spread through Sirhind and the Doáb to Delhí and
its dependent districts, and reduced them and the villages to a
miserable condition. Now it has wholly subsided. It is said by
old men, and it is also clear from the histories of former times,
that this disease had never appeared before in this country. I
asked the physicians and learned men what was the cause of it,
as for two years in succession the country had suffered from
famine, and there had been a deficiency of rain. Some said
that it was to be attributed to the impurity of the air arising
from drought and scarcity; but some ascribed it to other causes.
God knows, and we must patiently submit to his will.[1]

Before this date, some thieves had plundered the public
treasury of the *kotwáli*, and after a few days seven vagabonds
were apprehended, with their chief named Namal. Some of
the treasure was also recovered. I was incensed at the bold
conduct of these scoundrels, and consequently I was determined
to punish them severely. Each of them got a fitting punish-

---

[1] [A few pages before, and in the tenth year of his reign, Jahángír records that one
of his nobles died in the Dakhin of cholera (*haiza*).]

ment, and their chief was ordered to be trodden under the feet of an elephant. He petitioned to me that he would rather fight with that formidable animal than suffer the agony of being trampled under his feet. I consented to this. A dagger was given to him, and notwithstanding that the elephant, which was wild and vicious, prostrated him several times, and notwithstanding he had been witness to the fate of his associates, yet, with undaunted courage, he managed to recover his feet, and inflict several wounds with his dagger upon the trunk, and succeeded in driving the animal back. It was truly an act of wonderful bravery, and I therefore spared his life, directing at the same time he was to be taken care of. After some time, he ungratefully made his escape. It gave me much annoyance. I issued orders to the *jágírdárs* of the neighbourhood for his apprehension, and when caught he was hanged by the neck.

On the afternoon of Saturday, the 1st of Zí-l ka'da, corresponding with 21st of Ábán, I marched in sound health from Ajmír in a European carriage drawn by four horses, and I ordered several nobles to make up carriages similar to it,[1] and to attend upon me with them. About sunset I reached my camp in the village Deo Ráná, a distance of nearly two *kos*.[2]

It is customary in India, when a king, prince, or noble undertakes an expedition towards the east, to ride on an elephant with

---

[1] A little above he tells us, that on the departure of Bábá Khurram, he had given him "a carriage of the Feringí English fashion, that he might sit and ride in it." These are the only remote allusions made throughout the work to the embassy of Sir T. Roe, whose residence in Jahángír's camp lasted from the 10th January, 1616, to the 21st January, 1618.

[2] Sir Thomas Roe thus mentions the mode of departure from Ajmír : " Thus richly accoutred, the King went into the coach, which waited for him under the care of his new English servant, who was dressed as gaudily as any player, and more so, and had trained four horses for the draught, which were trapped and harnessed all in gold. This was the first coach he had ever been in, made in imitation of that sent from England, and so like it that I only knew the difference by the cover, which was of gold velvet of Persia. * * * Next followed the English coach, newly covered and richly trimmed, which he had given to his favourite queen, Nourmahal, who sat in the inside. After this came a coach made after the fashion of the country, which I thought seemed out of countenance, in which were his younger sons. This was followed by about twenty spare royal elephants, all for the King's own use."— (Kerr's *Collection of Voyages and Travels*, vol. ix. p. 312.)

long tusks; when towards the west, to ride on a horse of one
colour ; when towards the north, to go in a litter or *pálki ;* when
towards the south, to go in a carriage drawn by bullocks.   I
remained at Ajmír five days less than three years.   At that place
there is the holy shrine of Khwája Mu'ínu-d dín.   Ajmír is
situated within the limits of the second climate. * * *

A large tray of fruits was brought before me.   Among them
were the celebrated melons of Kárez, Badakhshán, and Kábul.
Grapes from the latter place as well as from Samarkand.   The
sweet pomegranates of Yazd, and the subacid ones of Farráh.
Pears from Samarkand and Badakhshán.   Apples from Kashmír,
Kábul, Jalálábád, and Samarkand were also there.   Pine-apples
from the seaports of the Europeans were also in the tray.   There
were some plants of this latter fruit placed in my private gardens
at Ágra, and after some time they produced several thousands
of that fruit.   The *kaulá* was also among them, which is smaller
than an orange, and full of sweet juice.   In the province of
Bengal it is produced in abundance.   I had no sufficient words
to thank Almighty God for the enjoyment of these delicious
fruits.   My father the late King was exceedingly fond of fruit,
especially melons, pomegranates, and grapes ; but in his reign,
the melons from Kárez, which are of the best quality, the pomegranates from Yazd, which are celebrated all over the world,
and pears from Samarkand, were never brought to India, and,
therefore, when I see and enjoy those luxuries, I regret that my
father is not here to share them. * * *

When I was Prince, I had promised to give an *Altamghá*
grant of the district of Málda in Bengal to Mír Ziáu-d dín, a
saiyid of Kazwín, and two of his sons.   When I ascended the
throne, I gave him the name of Mustafá Khán, and in this
journey I had the pleasure of fulfilling my promise. * * *

Mandú.

Mandú is one of the divisions of the province of Málwa, and
the total of its revenue is one *kror* thirty-nine *lacs* of *dáms.*

The city was for a long time the capital of the kings of this country. Many buildings and relics of the old kings are still standing, for as yet decay has not fallen upon the city. On the 24th, I rode out to see the royal edifices. First I visited the *jámi' masjid* which was built by Sultán Hoshang Ghorí. It is a very lofty building, and erected entirely of hewn stone. Although it has been standing 180 years, it looks as if built to-day.

Afterwards I visited the sepulchres of the kings and rulers of the Khiljí dynasty, among which there is also the tomb of the eternally cursed Nasiru-d dín, son of Sultán Ghiyásu-d dín. It is notorious that this graceless wretch twice attempted to kill his father by poison when he was in the eightieth year of his age; but the old monarch saved his life by the use of bezoar. The third time he gave him, with his own hand, a cup of sherbet mixed with poison, and told him that he must drink it. The father, seeing his son's determination, took the bezoar off his arm, and placed it before him. Then he bowed in humble supplication before his Maker, and said, " O Lord ! I have now arrived at the age of eighty. All this time I have passed in ease and prosperity, and in a state of pleasure such as has been the lot of no monarch. This moment is my last, and I pray thee not to hold my son Nasír answerable for my blood. May my death be deemed a natural death, and may my son be not held answer- for it." Having said this, he drank the poisoned draught and expired. What he meant by saying that he had enjoyed such luxury and pleasure as no king ever did was this: In the forty-eighth year of his age, when he succeeded to the throne, he said to his friends and associates, that in the time of his father he had spent thirty years of his life in the command of the army, and had done all that was required of a soldier. Now that the sovereignty had devolved upon him, he had no desire for con-quest, his only wish was to pass the remainder of his life in pleasure and luxury. It is said that he had 15,000 women in his harem. He built a city which was inhabited only by women, and all arts and sciences were taught them. The posts of governor, judge, magistrate, and all offices required in the management of a city, were held by persons of the female sex. Whenever he heard of a girl possessing beauty, he never rested till he obtained her. He was exceedingly fond of sport, and had made a deer park, in which he had collected all kinds of animals. He often amused himself in hunting in this park, in the company of women. As he had from the first determined, he made no invasion during his whole reign of thirty-two years, and spent all this time in ease, enjoyment, and pleasure; and no enemy made any attack upon his dominions.

It is reported that Sher Khán Afghán, in the course of his reign, came to the tomb of Nasíru-d dín, and although he had a brutal disposition, yet on account of the shameful deed above stated, he ordered his people to beat the tomb with their sticks. When I went to the tomb, I also kicked it several times, and ordered my attendants also to spurn it with their feet. Not satisfied even with this, I ordered the tomb to be opened, and the remains of that foul wretch to be thrown into fire. But then I remembered that fire is a part of the eternal light, and that it was very wrong to pollute it with that filthy matter. I also hesitated from burning his remains, lest by so doing a remission be made in his punishment in the next world. I ordered that his decayed bones and the dust of his body should be thrown into the Nerbudda, because it is said that as he had a very hot temper in the days of his youth, he always remained in water. It is well known that one day, in a fit of intoxication, he threw himself into the tank of Kaliyádah, which was very deep. Some of the servants of the palace caught hold of his hair and dragged him out. When he came to his senses, and learnt what had happened, and that they had dragged him out by the hair, he was so angry with them that he ordered their hands to be cut off. The next time he fell into the tank, nobody attempted to pull him out, and so he was drowned. Now, at a period of 110 years after his death, it had come to pass that his rotten remains were also mixed with water.

One night I turned the discourse of my courtiers on the chase, and told them how fond of it I formerly was. At the same time it occurred to my mind whether all the animals and birds which I had killed since the time of my coming to reason could not be calculated. I therefore ordered all the news-writers, the gamekeepers and other officers to ascertain and write out a list of all the various animals and birds I had killed, and to show it to me. Accordingly a paper was prepared, from which it appeared that from the twelfth year of my age, A.H. 988, to the end of the last year, the eleventh of my reign, and the fiftieth lunar year of my age, 28,532 animals and birds were killed in the course of my sport, of which 17,168 were graminivorous animals and birds I had shot or killed with my own hands, and the following is a detailed account of them.[1]

TWELFTH YEAR OF THE REIGN.

The Nau-roz of my twelfth year corresponded with 12th Rabí'u-l awwal, 1026 (10th March, 1617 A.D.).

Prohibition of Tobacco.

As the smoking of tobacco had taken very bad effect upon the health and mind of many persons, I ordered that no one should practise the habit. My brother Sháh 'Abbás, also being aware of its evil effects, had issued a command against the use of it in Írán. But Khán-i 'Álam was so much addicted to smoking, that he could not abstain from it, but oftened smoked.

Prince Khurram at Court.

On Thursday, the 20th Mihr, and the twelfth year of my reign, corresponding to the 11th of Shawwal, A.H. 1026, at about three o'clock after noon, Prince Khurram arrived and obtained audience in the fort of Mandú. He had been absent from the Court for eleven months and eleven days. After he had paid me his respects, I called him in the window where I was sitting, and

[1] [Sir H. M. Elliot gives a summary of it in a note, *infra*.]

with the impulse of excessive paternal affection and love, I immediately rose up and took him in my arms. The more he expressed his reverence and respect for me, the more my tenderness increased towards him. I ordered him to sit by me. He presented me with 1000 gold *mohurs* and 1000 rupees. * *

Formerly at the conquest of the Ráná, a *mansab* of 20,000 and the command of 10,000 horse had been conferred on Prince Khurram, and when he was sent to the Dakhin, he was honoured with the title of a Sháh. Now, in consideration of his present service, his *mansab* was promoted to a *mansab* of 30,000 and the command of 20,000 horse. I also conferred on him the title of Sháh-Jahán. It was also ordered, that henceforth a chair should be placed for him in the Court next to my throne, an honour which was particularly conferred on him, and had never before been known in my family.

A report came from Kashmír, that in the house of a silk-dealer two girls were born who had teeth in their mouths, and who were joined together by the back as far as the waist,[1] but their heads, hands, and feet were all separate. They lived only a little time, and then died.

On Monday, the 2nd of the month, I drank wine in an assembly at the banks of a tank where my tents were pitched.[2]

Journey to Gujarát.

On Friday, the 1st of De, I marched three *kos* and three-quarters, and encamped on the banks of the tank of Jhanúd. At this place Rái Mán, the head of the royal footmen, caught a Rahú fish and brought it to me. I was very fond of this fish, which is the best of all the fishes found in India. Since the date I had passed the defile of Chándá up to this time, a space of eleven months, I had not been able to procure it, although every search was made. I was highly pleased at receiving it this day, and granted Rái Mán a horse.

[1] از پشت تا کمر باهم متصل

[2] [This is but one of many similar entries.]

Though the country from the *pargana* of Dahad is reckoned as
belonging to Gujarát, yet it was only from this stage that I saw
a marked difference in all things, both jungle and cultivation.
The people and their tongue were different. The jungles which
I saw on the roadside were full of fruit trees, such as those of
the mango, khirní, and tamarind. The fields are protected by
the thorns of the zakúm tree. The cultivators, in order to
separate the lands of their respective possessions, make hedges of
these thorns round their fields, and between them leave a narrow
path for wayfarers. As the soil is very sandy, the least movement in a party of travellers raises so much dust, that one can
see another's face with difficulty, and therefore it came into my
mind, that thenceforth Ahmadabád should not be called by that
name, but Gardábád.

Kambay.

On Friday we travelled a distance of six *kos* and a half, and
the tents were pitched on the sea-shore. Khambáit (Kambay)
is a very ancient port, and according to the Brahmins many
thousand years have elapsed since its foundation. In the beginning it was called Trimbáwatí, and Rájá Nar Singh Makhwár was
its ruler. It would be very tedious to detail the account of this
Rájá as given by the Brahmins. To be brief, when the chiefship
devolved on Rájá Abhí Kumár, who was a descendant of his, by
the will of heaven a great calamity fell upon this city. A shower
of dust and dirt fell, and buried all the houses and buildings, and
destroyed a great number of people. Before the occurrence of
this catastrophe, an idol, which the Rájá used to worship, appeared to him in a dream, and informed him of the approaching
misfortune. Consequently, he embarked with his family on a
vessel, and he also took with him the idol and the pillar which
supported it behind. It so happened that the vessel was battered
by a storm; but as the Rájá was destined to live some time
longer, he, by means of that same pillar, brought the ship and
himself safe to land. He then set up that pillar as a mark of

his intention to rebuild and newly people the place. As a pillar in Hindí is called Khamb, the city was hence called Khambáwatí, which was gradually worn down by constant use into Khambáit. This port is one of the largest in Hindústán, and is situated on one of the estuaries of the sea of 'Umán. The average breadth of this estuary is estimated to be seven *kos*, and the length about forty. Ships cannot enter this branch, but are anchored in the port of Goga, which is one of the dependencies of Khambáit, and is near the high sea. From hence the cargoes are transported to Khambáit on boats (*gharáb*, grabs), and in the same manner merchandize intended for exportation is carried to the ships. Before the arrival of my victorious arms, several boats had come to Khambáit from the ports of Europe, and the crews, after selling and purchasing goods, were on the point of returning. On Sunday, the 10th, having decorated their boats, they displayed them before me, and then took their departure towards their destination. On Monday, the 11th, I embarked on a boat, and sailed about one *kos*.

In the time of the Sultáns of Gujarát, the *tamghá* or customs duty levied from the merchants was very large; but it is now ordered that no more than one part in forty should be taken. In other ports the custom officers[1] take the tenth or twentieth part, and give all sorts of trouble and annoyance to the merchants and travellers. In Jedda, the port of Mecca, one-fourth is taken, and sometimes even more than that; hence it may be inferred what the duties at the ports of Gujarát were in former reigns. Thanks be to God, this humble creature of the Almighty has dispensed with levying the *tamghá*, which amounted to a sum beyond calculation, throughout the territories under his rule, and the very name of *tamghá* has disappeared from his dominions.

Coins.

It was also ordered in these days, that *tankas* of gold and silver, ten and twenty times heavier than the current gold

---

[1] ['*Ushúrgas*, literally, tithing-men.]

mohur and rupee, should be struck.[1] The legend on the face
of the golden *tanka* was "Jahángír Sháh, A.H. 1027," and on
the reverse, "Struck at Khambáit, the 12th year of H. M.
reign." For the silver *tanka*, on one side, "Jahángír Sháh, A.H.
1027," with a verse round it, the meaning of which is, "This
coin was struck by Jahángír Sháh, the ray of victory." On the
other side was impressed, "Struck at Khambáit, the 12th year
of H. M. reign," with this verse round it, "After the conquest
of the Dakhin, he came from Mándú to Gujarát." In no reign
before this had *tankas* been coined except of copper. The *tankas*
of gold and silver were inventions of my own, and I called them
Jahángiri tankas.[2]

Conquest of Khúrda.

Intelligence arrived from the eastern provinces that Mukarram
Khán, son of Mu'azzam Khán, who had been appointed to the
governorship of Orissa, had conquered the territory of Khúrda;
and that its Rájá had sought protection at the Court of
Rájá Mahendra. As a reward of this service, the Khán was
favoured with a *mansab* of 3000 personal allowance and the command of 2000 horse. He was also honoured with a kettle-drum,
a horse, and a *khil'at*. Between the province of Orissa and
Golkonda, there were the territories of two *zamíndárs*, viz. the
Rájá of Khúrda and the Rájá Mahendra. The territories of the
former have been taken possession of by the servants of my
Government, and it is hoped that through the influence of the
Emperor's prosperous star, that of the latter will also be soon
added to the protected countries.

---

[1] In the sixteenth year of the reign, he gives to the Persian ambassador a gold
mohur, called *Núr-jahání*, weighing 100 *tolas*. In the twelfth year, he gives to the
vakíls of 'Ádil Khán a gold *mohur*, called *kaukab tola*, equal to 500 current gold *mohurs*.
In the tenth year he gives one of the same weight to the ambassador of 'Ádil Khán,
but calls it a *Núr-jahání*.

[2] [This statement is certainly not true, so far as regards the silver *tanka*; and it
seems to have puzzled the copyists, for in several MSS. the word سیم (I) is written
instead of مس (copper), making the whole passage unintelligible. But perhaps
nonsense was preferred to error.]

The Jám of Gujarát.

When the royal tents were pitched on the banks of the Mahí, the *zamíndár* (called) Jám attended at Court. Having obtained the honour of kissing the ground, he presented fifty horses, 100 *mohurs*, and 100 rupees. His name was Jasá, and Jám was his title, which is held by every man who succeeds to the chiefship. He is one of the greatest *zamíndárs* of the province of Gujarát. His territory is bordered by the sea. He has always 5000 or 6000 horsemen; but in time of war he can collect 10,000 or 12,000. There are plenty of excellent horses in his territory, and a Kachí horse is sold at as high as 2000 or 3000 rupees. I bestowed a *khil'at* upon him.

THIRTEENTH YEAR OF THE REIGN.

On Sunday night, the 23rd of Rabí'u-l awwal, A.H. 1027 (10th March, 1618), at about two hours after sunset, that great luminary which benefits the world with its bounty entered Aries, the first sign of the Zodiac. This New Year's Day which gave light to the world, brought to a close the twelfth year of this humble servant of God, which had been passed in happiness, and now a new, auspicious and prosperous year began.

On Thursday, the 2nd of Farwardín, the festival of my being weighed against metals on the lunar anniversary of my birth occurred ; and the happy fifty-first year of my age commenced. May the remaining days of my life be spent in occupations consistent with the will of God, and no moment pass without reflection upon his goodness ! After the ceremony was over, a wine party was convened, and the most familiar servants of the throne, being favoured with draughts of wine, became merry.

The Tuesday night, 21st of the month, I marched on my return towards Ahmadábád. As the excess of heat and the oppressive atmosphere were very grievous to the camp followers, and a great distance had to be travelled before we could reach Ágra, it occurred to me that I had better remain at Mándú during this hot season. As I had heard much praise of the rainy season of Gujarát.

and as there was no comparison between the city of Ahmadábád and that of Mándú, I at last determined to remain in the former. The Almighty God always and in all places has extended his assistance and protection to this his humble creature; and this is shown from the fact that at this very time it was reported to me that a pestilential disease (*wabá*) had broken out in Ágra, and numbers of men had perished. For this reason I was fully confirmed in my resolution of postponing my march towards Ágra, which had occurred to my mind by the divine inspiration.

Coins.

Formerly it was customary to strike my name on one side of the coin, and that of the place, and the month, and the year of the reign, on the obverse. It now occurred to my mind that, instead of the name of the month, the figure of the sign of the Zodiac corresponding to the particular month should be stamped. For instance, in the month of Farwardín the figure of a Ram, in Urdíbihisht that of a Bull, and so on ; that is, in every month in which a coin might be struck, the figure of the constellation in which the Sun might be at the time should be impressed on one side of it. This was my own innovation. It had never been done before.

Drinking.

On Thursday, 20,000 *darabs* were granted to Hakím Masíhu-z Zamán, and 100 gold *mohurs* and 1000 rupees to Hakím Rúhu-lla. As they well knew that the air of Gujarát was very uncongenial to my health, they told me that if I would diminish a little the usual quantity of wine and opium which I took, my complaint would be at once removed. Accordingly, on the very first day I derived great benefit from their advice.

Illness of Jahángír.

On Saturday I had a severe headache, which was followed by fever. That night I did not take my usual quantity of wine. After midnight the effect of my abstinence became apparent, and aggravated the fever with which I was tossing about on my bed till morning. In the evening of Sunday the fever decreased ; and by the advice of some physicians of Multán, I took my usual quantity of wine. They also repeatedly recommended me to take some gruel made of pulse and rice, but I could not manage to do so. From the time I arrived at years of discretion, I had never, so far as I recollect, drunk such broth, and I hope I may never be obliged to drink it again. When my meal was brought, I had no inclination to take it. In short, I fasted altogether three days and three nights. Although I had fever only one day and one night, yet I was as weak as if I had been for a long time laid up in my bed. I had no appetite at all.

Ahmadábád.

I am at a loss to conceive what beauty and excellence the founder of this city saw in this wretched land, that he was induced to build a city here ; and how after him others also should spend the days of their precious life in this dirty place. Hot wind always blows here, and there is very little water. I have already mentioned that it is very sandy, and that the atmosphere is loaded with dust. The water is exceedingly bad and disagreeable ; and the river which runs along the outskirts of the city is always dry, except during the rains. The water of the wells is bitter and brackish, and that of the tanks in the outskirts becomes like buttermilk from the mixture of soap which the washermen leave in it. Those people who are somewhat affluent have reservoirs in their houses, which are filled with rain-water during the rainy season, and they drink from this supply during the whole year. It is manifestly very injurious to drink water which is never fanned by a breeze, and stagnates in a place where there is no passage for exhalation. Outside of the city, instead of verdure and flowers, all the ground is covered with *zakúm* (thorn-trees), and the effect of the air which blows over these thorns is well known. I have previously called this city Gardábád. Now I do not know what to call it—whether Samúmistán (the home of the simoom), Bímáristán (place of sickness), Zakúmdár (thorn-brake), or Jahannamábád (hell), for all these names are appropriate.

Poetry.

It was reported in these days that Khán-khánán, the commander-in-chief and my preceptor, had composed a *ghazal* in imitation of the well-known verse—

"For one rose the pain of a hundred thorns must be suffered."

And that Mírza Rustam Safawí and Mírza Murád his son had also tried their talents in the same manner. Instantly the following couplet occurred to my mind—

"A cup of wine should be quaffed in the presence of one's beloved.
The clouds too are thick, it is time to drink deep."

Of my courtiers who were present, those who had a turn for poetry composed *ghazals* and repeated them before me. The first-mentioned verse is a very celebrated one, composed by Mauláná 'Abdu-r Rahmán Jámí. I have read the whole *ghazal*; but except that verse, which is, as it were, a proverb on the tongues of all people, the others are not of any great elegance. They are, indeed, very plain and homely.

Pictures.

This day Abú-l Hasan, a painter, who bore the title of Nádiru-z Zamán, drew a picture of my Court, and presented it to me. He had attached it as a frontispiece to the *Jahángír-náma*. As it was well worthy of praise, I loaded him with great favours. He was an elegant painter, and had no match in his time. If the celebrated artists Abú-l Hai and Bihzád were now alive, they would do him full justice for his exquisite taste in painting. His father, Áka Razá, was always with me while I was a Prince, and his son was born in my household. However, the son is far superior to the father. I gave him a good education, and took care to cultivate his mind from his youth till he became one of

the most distinguished men of his age. The portraits furnished
by him were beautiful. Mansúr is also a master of the art of
drawing, and he has the title of Nádiru-l Aslí. In the time of
my father and my own, there have been none to compare with
these two artists. I am very fond of pictures, and have such
discrimination in judging them, that I can tell the name of the
artist, whether living or dead. If there were similar portraits
finished by several artists, I could point out the painter of each.
Even if one portrait were finished by several painters, I could
mention the names of those who had drawn the different portions
of that single picture. In fact, I could declare without fail by
whom the brow and by whom the eye-lashes were drawn, or if
any one had touched up the portrait after it was drawn by the
first painter.[1]

Publication of the Emperor's Memoirs.

As the events of twelve years forming part of the *Jahángír-
náma* had been written down, I ordered the *mutasaddis* of my
library to make a volume of them, and prepare a number of
copies, to be distributed among the chief servants of the throne,
and also to be sent to all parts of the country, that great and
influential men might make it their study and exemplar. On
Friday, one of my writers having finished a copy and bound it,
brought it to me. As this was the first copy, I gave it to Prince
Sháh Jahán, whom I considered in all things the first of all my
sons. On the outside of it I wrote with my own hand that it was
presented to him on such a date and at such a place. May he
be favoured with the ability of knowing the contents of it,
which shall obtain for him God's grace and the blessings of His
creatures!

---

[1] "In his time there were found, in the Indies, native painters, who copied the
finest of our European pictures with a fidelity that might vie with the originals. He
was partial to the sciences of Europe, and it was this which attached him to the
Jesuits. He caused a church and a residence to be built for them at Lahore."—
Catrou's *History of the Mogul Dynasty*, p. 178. See also Sir T. Roe in Kerr's
Collection of Voyages and Travels, vol. ix. pp. 279-289.

Executions.

At this date a certain prisoner was brought before me, and I gave orders for his execution. The executioner acted very promptly, carried him to the place of punishment, and gave effect to my order. After a little while, at the intercession of one of my courtiers, I granted his life, but ordered his feet to be cut off. But according to his destiny, he had been beheaded before my orders arrived. Although he deserved death, yet I regretted the circumstance, and ordered that henceforth, in the event of any person being sentenced to death, notwithstanding that the orders might be imperative, yet they should not be carried into effect till sunset, and if up to that time no reprieve should be issued, the punishment should be then inflicted on the criminal.

A Bázár at Court.

On Tuesday night, the 19th, a bázár was held at my own residence. Before this, it was an established custom that the sellers of manufactured goods of the city should bring and expose them for sale in the courtyard of my palace. Jewels, inlaid articles, implements, and all kinds of cloths and stuffs sold in the bázárs, were to be seen on these occasions. It came into my mind, that if the market were held in the night-time, and plenty of lanterns were lighted before each shop, it would be a very pretty exhibition. In fact, when it was done, it was exactly as I had anticipated; it was altogether a novelty. I visited all the shops, and purchased what jewels and ornamented articles and other things appeared good to me.

Drinking.

The climate of this part of the country was not beneficial to my health, and the physicians had advised me to lessen the quantity of wine I usually drank. I deemed this prudent, and began to do so. In the course of one week I reduced the quantity about one cup. Formerly I took six cups every night, each cup containing seven *tolas* and a half of liquor, that is, forty-five *tolas* altogether;[1] but now each cup contained six and one-third of a *tola*, the whole being thirty-seven *tolas* and a half.

Renunciation of Hunting.

It was one of the remarkable events of my life, that when I was about sixteen or seventeen years, I made at Allahábád a vow to God, that when I should arrive at the fiftieth year of my age, I would leave off shooting, and give no pain to any living creature.[2] Mukarrab Khán, who was one of my most confidential officers, was acquainted with this vow. In short, now that I had arrived at that age, and the fiftieth year had commenced, one day it happened, that through the excess of smoke and vapour, I could not freely draw my breath, and was very much troubled on that account. In this state I suddenly, through divine inspiration, recollected what I had promised, and now I determined to conform to my former resolution. I resolved within myself, that after the lapse of this the fiftieth year, and the expiration of the time I had fixed, I would, under the guidance of Almighty God, go to visit the tomb of my father, and, having invoked the aid of his holy soul, I would entirely abstain from that habit. As soon as these ideas occurred to my mind, I was entirely relieved of pain, and found myself fresh and happy. I immediately indulged my tongue by expressing thanks to the Almighty God, and I trusted that he would assist me in my resolution.[3]

---

[1] [Rather more than an Imperial pint.]

[2] His passion for shooting is shown by the statement which he makes at the close of the events of the eleventh year. He there says that as the discourse happened one night to turn upon sport, he directed his news-writers and huntsmen to make out a statement, showing how many animals he had killed during his life. It appeared that he had been present, from the twelfth year of his age to his fiftieth, at the death of no less than 28,532 animals, of which 17,168 had been killed with his own hand, *i.e.*, 3203 quadrupeds, comprising, amongst others, 86 tigers, 889 *nilgáos*, 1372 deer, 36 wild buffaloes, 90 wild boars, 23 hares; and 13,964 birds, including 10,348 pigeons, and 156 waterfowl. The number is made up of crows, owls, doves, and other birds, which do not enter into the catalogue of English sport.

[3] [The Emperor subsequently retracted his resolution, and gives his reason for so doing; but it is not consistent with what is here stated to be the cause of his resolve; see *infrà*, p. 384. He frequently went out hunting. In the eighteenth year of his reign, and fifty-sixth of his age, he records that he went out on horseback and shot a tiger]

A Bridge.

In the next march I crossed the Mahí by the bridge which had been thrown over it. Although in this river there were no boats fit for building bridges, and the water was very deep and flowed forcibly, yet through the good management of Abú-l Hasan Mír Bakhshí, a very strong bridge of 140 yards in length and four yards in breadth was prepared in only three days. By way of testing its strength, I ordered one of my largest elephants with three other female elephants to be taken over it. The bridge was so strong that the weight of the mountain-like elephants did not shake it in the least.

A Comet.[1]

Saturday, 17th *Zi-l ka'da*. Several nights before this, a little before dawn, a luminous vapour, in the form of a column, had made its appearance, and every succeeding night it arose half an hour earlier than on the preceding night. When it had attained its full development, it looked like a spear[2] with the two ends thin, but thick about the middle. It was a little curved like a reaping-sickle, with its back towards the south, and its edge towards the north. On the date above mentioned, it rose three hours before sunrise. The astronomers measured its size with their astrolabes, and, on an average of different observations, it was found to extend 24 degrees. Its course was in the empyrean heaven, but it had a proper motion of its own, independent of that firmament, as it was retrograde—first appearing in the sign of the Scorpion, then in that of the Scales. Its declination was southerly. Astrologers call such a phenomenon a spear, and have written that it portends evil to the chiefs of Arabia, and the establishment of an enemy's power over them. God only knows if this be true !

Sixteen nights[3] after its first appearance, a comet appeared in

---

[1] [This passage is the work of Sir H. M. Elliot.]

[2] This word might also be translated a "porcupine."

[3] Literally, "Up to the above date after sixteen nights since the phenomenon a .e," to which it is difficult to assign any exact meaning.

the same quarter, having a shining nucleus, with a tail in appearance about two or three yards long, but in the tail there was no light or splendour. Up to the present time, nearly eight years have elapsed since its first appearance, and when it disappears, I shall take care to record it, as well as the effects which have resulted from it.[1]

A Story.

On the way I passed through a field of *juwár*, in which every plant had no less than twelve bunches of corn, while in other fields there is generally only one. It excited my astonishment, and recalled to my mind the tale of the King and the Gardener. A King entered a garden during the heat of the day, and met a gardener there. He inquired of him whether there were any pomegranates, and received a reply that there were. His Majesty told him to bring a cupful of the juice of that fruit, on which the gardener told his daughter to execute that commission. She was a handsome and accomplished girl. She brought the cupful of that beverage, and covered it with a few leaves. The King drank it, and asked the girl why she had put the leaves over it. The girl with much readiness replied, that she had done it to prevent His Majesty drinking too fast, as drinking of liquids just after a fatiguing journey was not good. The King fell in love with her, and wished to take her into his palace. He asked the gardener how much he derived each year from his garden. He said 300 *dinárs*. He then asked how much he paid to the

---

[1] It was the discovery of a similar phenomenon, namely a new star in Cassiopeia, not fifty years before this, which introduced Tycho Brahe to the notice of the world as an astronomer. The star he discovered, however, only lasted from November, 1572, to March, 1574. The greatest of Grecian astronomers, Hipparchus, is said to have become an observer through the discovery of a similar phenomenon. As Jahángir's star, if it was one, appeared in the Ecliptic, it must have been noticed by European astronomers, especially as the discoveries effected by Galileo's telescope were at that time attracting general observation to the heavens. The statement given in the Extract from the *Ikbál-náma* is much more probable than this. In that there is no mention of its continuance, and merely the effects which were visible for eight years are recorded, according to the superstitious notions of the time.

diwán. He gave answer that he did not pay anything on fruit-trees, b' t whatever sum he derived from his agriculture, he paid a tenth part to the State. His Majesty said within himself, "There are numerous gardens and trees in my dominions; and if I fix a revenue of a tenth on them, I shall collect a great deal of money." He then desired the girl to bring another cup of the pomegranate juice. She was late in bringing it this time, and it was not much she brought. His Majesty asked her the reason for this deficiency, observing that she brought it quickly the first time and in great plenty, that now she had delayed long, and brought but little. The daughter replied, "The first time one pomegranate sufficed. I have now squeezed several, and have not been able to obtain so much juice." The Sultán was astonished, upon which her father replied that good produce is entirely dependent on the good disposition of the Sovereign; that he believed that his guest was a King; and that from the time he inquired respecting the produce of the garden, his disposition was altogether changed; and that therefore the cup did not come full of the juice. The Sultán was impressed with his remark, and resolved upon relinquishing the tax. After a little time, His Majesty desired the girl to bring a third cup of the same beverage. This time the girl came sooner, and with a cup brimful, which convinced the King that the surmise of the gardener was sound. The Sultán commended the gardener's penetration, and divulged to him his real rank, and the reflections which had been passing in his mind. He then asked to be allowed to take his daughter in marriage, in order that a memorial of this interview and its circumstances might remain for the instruction of the world. In short, the abundance of produce depends entirely on the good will and justice of the Sovereign. Thanks to the Almighty God, that no revenue on fruit-trees has been taken during my reign; and I gave orders that if any one were to plant a garden in cultivated land, he was not to pay any revenue. I pray that the Almighty may cause the mind of this humble creature to entertain good and pure intentions!

Ranthambor.

On Monday, the 3rd De, I went to see the fort of Ranthambor. There are two hills adjacent to each other, one is called Ran, and the other Thambor, and the fort stands on the latter. The name of Ranthambor is formed by the connexion of the two names. Although the fort is very strong, and has much water in it, yet the hill called Ran is still stronger and better situated, and the fort can be taken only from that side.

FOURTEENTH YEAR OF THE REIGN.

[The *Nau-roz* of my fourteenth year corresponded with — Rabí'u-l ákhir, 1028 н. (10th March, 1619 A.D.).]

Núr Jahán shoots a Tiger.

[My huntsmen reported to me that there was in the neighbour-hood (of Mathurá) a tiger, which greatly distressed the inhabitants. I ordered his retreat to be closely surrounded with a number of elephants. Towards evening I and my attendants mounted and went out. As I had made a vow not to kill any animal with my own hands, I told Núr Jahán to fire my musket. The smell of the tiger made the elephant very restless, and he would not stand still, and to take good aim from a *howda* is a very difficult feat. Mírza Rustam, who after me has no equal as a marksman, has fired three or four shots from an elephant's back without effect. Núr Jahán, however, killed this tiger with the first shot.]

'Abdú-l Hakk Dehlawi.

[Shaikh 'Abdú-l Hakk Dehlawi,[1] one of the most learned and accomplished men of the time, came to wait upon me, and presented to me a book which he had written upon the *h-ikhs* of India. He had suffered a good deal of trouble, and was living in retirement at Dehlí, resigned to his lot and trusting in God. He was an excellent man, and his society was very agreeable. I showed him great attention and courtesy.]

[1] [See *supr'd*, p. 175.]

Journey to Kashmír.

[1] On Tuesday, the 14th, the royal camp halted at Hasan Abdál. As an account of this road and a description of the stages have been already given in the narrative of my expedition to Kábul, I will not repeat them here; but from this place to Kashmír I will record all occurrences, stage by stage, please God! From the time of my disembarking from boats at Akbarpúr up to reaching Hasan Abdál, I have travelled 178 *kos* during sixty-nine days, in fifty-eight marches and one halt. As there are at this place a fountain, a small cascade, and a basin filled with water of the most translucent clearness, I remained here two days.

On Thursday, the 16th, I celebrated the lunar anniversary, and the fifty-second lunar year of my age commenced, in all gratitude to my Maker, and with every prospect of happiness. As the road I was going to take was full of hills and passes, ravines and ascents, and the royal party would have found it difficult to march all together, it was determined that the lady Maryamu-z Zamání, and the other *begams*, should remain behind a few days, and come on at their ease afterwards; and the Prime Minister, I'timádu-d daula al-Khákání, Sádik Khán Bakhshí, and Sa'ádat Khán Mír Sámán, should also come on subsequently with the household and establishments. For the same reason Mírza Safawí and Khán-i 'Azam were sent on with a party of my attendants by way of Púnch, and I myself went accompanied by only a few of my personal friends, and the servants who were absolutely necessary.

On Friday I marched three *kos* and a half to Sultánpúr.[2] Here intelligence was received of Ráná Amar Singh having died a natural death. Jagat Singh, his grandson, and Bhím, his son, who were in attendance upon me, were honoured with *khil'ats*, and it was ordered that Rájá Kishan Dás should convey to Kunwar Karan a *farmán*, conferring the title of Ráná, with a

[1] [Translated by Sir H. M. Elliot.]
[2] This village lies on the southern bank of the Harroh river.

khil'at, and a horse from my own stables, and so do him honour, and congratulate him upon his succession.

I heard from the people of this country that a noise like that of thunder fell upon the ear from a hill in the neighbourhood, though there might be at the time no sign of rain, or cloud, or lightning. They therefore call this hill Garaj. This sound is now to be heard every year, or certainly every two years. I have also heard this matter frequently mentioned in my father's presence. As the story is a very strange one, I have recorded it, but God knows whether it is true.[1]

On Saturday, the 18th, I marched four *kos* and a half to Sahí. During this stage we entered the *pargana* of Hazára Fárígh.[2]

On Sunday, the 19th, we encamped at Naushehra,[3] after travelling three *kos* and three-quarters, where we entered Dhamtaur. As far as the eye could reach, the blossoms of the *thal kanwal* and other flowers were glowing between the green foliage. It was a beautiful scene.

On Monday, the 20th, after a march of three *kos* and a half, I arrived at Sálhar,[4] where Mahábat Khán presented jewels and inlaid arms to the value of 60,000 rupees. In this tract I saw

---

[1] This is still commonly reported in the neighbourhood, but the sounds are said to have ceased within the last twenty years, since the fort of Srihote was built on the summit of the hill. The mountain is no doubt that which is now called Gandgarh, composed of clay-slate capped with limestone. The name of Garaj is not now known, but the local tradition is, that it was once called Ganjgarh (evidently Garajgarh), but that some Emperor changed it to Gandgarh "the bald," on account of its apparent barrenness. The sounds are said to proceed from a Rákas, or demon, whom Rájá Rasálu, the King Arthur of the traditions of the Upper Sind Ságar, imprisoned in a cavern. He was the son of Sálbában, and is said to have built the tope at Phallúr, near Usmán Khátur.

[2] Hazára is not so called from the famous Mughal tribe, as there are none of them in it. The fertility of this valley is celebrated especially for wheat. A local distich runs :—

"Chach Hazára kanaka bhalyán, Dhanne khúbí gáin ;
Súr Sikesar te ghore bhale, Ishnor doábe te dháen."

That is, the wheat of Chach Hazára, the cows of Dhanni, the horses of Sikesar (salt range), the rice of Hashtnagar (near Peshawar), are all excellent.

[3] The village is on the eastern bank of the river Dhor, but the distance between this place and Sultánpúr is greater than here represented.

[4] This place is on the eastern bank of one of the feeders of the same river, under Mount Sirban.

a flower red and fiery, in the form of a *gul khitmi* (marsh-mallow), but smaller. So many flowers were blooming near one another, that it appeared to be all one flower. The tree is like that of the apricot. On the slope of this hill there were many wild violets, of exceeding fragrance, but their colour was paler than that of the usual variety.

On Tuesday, the 21st, we travelled three *kos*, and encamped at Malgallí.[1] On this day Mahábat Khán was despatched to his government at Bangásh, and I gave him a *khil'at*, a *postín*, and an elephant from my private stables. During the whole march there was drizzling rain, and it rained also at night. Snow fell in the morning, and as the whole road was muddy and very slippery, the beasts which happened to be at all weak fell in every direction, and were not able to rise again. Twenty-five elephants belonging to the illustrious Government were lost upon the occasion. As the weather was very cloudy, I halted here for two days.

On Thursday, the 23rd, Sultán Husain, the *zamíndár* of Paklí (or Pakhali), obtained the honour of kissing the earth, for here we had entered Paklí. It is an extraordinary thing that, when my father was here, snow also fell as it did on this occasion; whereas for several years past there had been no fall, and rain also had been very scanty.

On Friday, the 24th, I marched four *kos* to Tawádkar. There was much mud on this road also, and the whole way the plum and guava trees were in blossom, and the pine-trees also were ravishing to the sight.

On Saturday, the 25th, I travelled over nearly three *kos* and a half to the neighbourhood of Paklí.

On Sunday, the 26th, I mounted and rode down some partridges.[2] Towards evening, at the request of Sultán Husain, I

---

[1] Still well known as an encamping ground, more generally called Mangli.

[2] "The Afgháns often ride down partridges in a way which is much easier of execution than one would imagine. Two or more horsemen put up a partridge, which makes a short flight and sits down; a horseman then puts it up again. The hunters

went to his residence, and honoured him much in the eyes of his
compeers and friends. My father also visited him. He presented
some horses, swords, hawks, and falcons. I accepted some of the
birds, and returned the other things.

Sarkár Paklí is thirty-five *kos* in length, by twenty-five in
breadth. On the east it has the mountains of Kashmír, on
the west Attock Benares, on the north Kator, on the south the
country of the Ghakkars. It is said that when Tímúr was
returning to Túrán from the conquest of Hindústán, he left some
of his followers here. The people themselves say they are by
origin Farsís (?), but they cannot tell what was the name of their
leader. They are now called Lahorí, and their speech is that of
the *Játs*. The same may be said of the people of Dhamtaur.
In the time of my father Sháh Rukh was the *zamíndár* of
Dhamtaur. His son Bahádur is now *zamíndár*. Although the
people of Paklí and Dhamtaur intermarry and communicate
freely, yet they are always quarrelling, like other *zamíndárs*,
about boundaries. These people have always been well affected
towards our family. Sultán Mahmúd, the father of Sultán
Husain of Paklí, and Sháh Rukh, both came to visit me before
my accession. Notwithstanding that Sultán Husain is seventy
years old, he is to all appearance strong; he can ride and take
exercise.

In this country *bozah* is prepared from bread and rice, which
liquor the people call *sir*, but it is very much stronger than *bozah*.
They drink nothing but *sir* with their food, and the oldest is
considered to be the best; and when the ingredients are mixed,
the people keep it tied up in jars for two or three years in their
houses. They then take off the scum, and the liquor is called
áchí, which can be kept for ten years. If it is kept for a longer
period, so much the better; but it should never be less than one
year old. Sultán Mahmúd used to take a cup of *sir*, and yet a

relieve one another, so as to allow the bird no rest, till it becomes too tired to fly,
when they ride it over as it runs, or knock it down with sticks."—Elphinstone's
Kingdom of Caubul, vol. i. p. 375.

mouthful is sufficient to create intoxication. Sultán Husain does the same. They brought the very first quality for my use. I took some by way of trial. I had taken some before. It is harsh and bitter to the taste; and it seems that they mix a little *bhang* in it. If you get drunk with it, it occasions drowsiness. If there were no such thing as wine, this might be used as a substitute. The fruits are apricots, peaches, and pears, but they are all sour and ill-flavoured.

They make their houses and dwellings all of wood, after the manner of Kashmir. There is plenty of game here, as well as horses, mules, and horned cattle. Goats and fowls are abundant. The mules are rendered weak and useless, in consequence of the heavy loads which they have been made to carry. As it was reported that a few marches ahead the country was not sufficiently populous to supply food for my retinue, orders were issued to take only the few tents and establishments which were absolutely necessary, to diminish the number of elephants, and to take supplies sufficient for three or four days. A few attendants were selected to accompany me, and the rest were placed under the orders of Khwája Abú-l Hasan Nakhshabí, to follow a few stages after me. Notwithstanding all my precautions and injunctions, it was found necessary to take with me 700 elephants even for the reduced tents and establishments. The *mansab* of Sultán Husain, which was 400 personal and 300 horse, was raised to 600 personal and 350 horse, and I gave him a *khil'at*, an ornamented dagger, and an elephant. Bahádur Dhamtaurí, who stands appointed to Bangash, was raised to a *mansab* of 200 personal and 100 horse.

On Sunday, the 29th, I marched five *kos* and a quarter, crossing the bridge and stream of Nain Sukh. This Nain Sukh flows from the north to the south, rising in the hills below the country of Badakhshán and Tibet. As in this place the river is divided into two branches, I ordered two wooden bridges to be made; one was eighteen yards long, and the other fourteen, and the breadth of each was five yards. The following is the mode of making a

bridge in this country. Trees of *sál* are thrown over the river,
and their two ends are lashed firmly to the rock; and across
these thick planks are riveted strongly with nails and ropes. A
bridge so made lasts for several years, with occasional repairs.
The elephants were made to ford the stream, but horse and foot
crossed over the bridge. It was Sultán Mahmúd who named
this river Nain Sukh, which means " the eye's repose."

On Thursday, the 3rd, after travelling nearly three *kos* and a
half, we encamped on the bank of the Kishengangá. On this
march we crossed an exceedingly high hill; the ascent was one
kos, and the descent one and a half. They call it Pham Dirang,
because in the Kashmírí tongue cotton is called *pham*, and as
there were agents here, on account of the Kings of Kashmír,
who levied duties on each load of cotton, and as delay or *dirang*
occurred on this account, the place became known as Pham
Dirang. After passing the bridge, we saw a cascade, of which
the water was beautifully clear. Sitting down near it, I drank my
usual cups of wine, and arrived in camp at eventide. There was
an old bridge over this river fifty-four yards long, and one and
a half broad, by which those on foot crossed. I ordered another
bridge to be made near it, fifty-three yards long and three broad.
As the stream was deep and rapid, I made the elephants pass
over without their loads, but horse and foot crossed by the
bridges. By orders of my father, a very strong *sarái* was built
here of stone and mortar, on the top of a hill to the east of the
river.

As only one day remained before the Sun would enter a new
sign, I sent on Mu'tamad Khán to select a high and conspicuous
spot on which to erect my throne, and make preparations for the
festival of the New Year. It so happened that a little beyond
the bridge, on the eastern bank of the river, there was an
eminence—a charming green spot, on the top of which there
was a level surface of fifty yards, just as if the executors of the
decrees of God had designed it for such an occasion. It was
there that Mu'tamad Khán set up the decorations for the

festival, and managed all so admirably as to call forth my praises and acknowledgments.

The river Kishenganga flows from the north towards the south.[1] The river Behat, flowing from the east, falls into the Kishenganga, taking a northerly course.[2]*

FIFTEENTH YEAR OF THE REIGN.

[The Nau-roz of the fifteenth year of my reign fell on the 15th Rabí'u-s sání, 1029 H. (10th March, 1620 A.D.).]

Kashmír.

On Friday, the 27th, I rode out to see the fountain of Vírnág, which is the source of the river Behat. I went five *kos* in a boat, and anchored near Mánpúr. This day I received very sad news from Kishtiwár. When Diláwar Khán, after the conquest of that country, returned to Court, he left Nasru-lla, an Arab, with several other officers, for the protection of the country. This man committed two faults of judgment. He oppressed the *zamíndárs* and the people, and he foolishly complied with the wishes of his troops, who petitioned him for leave to come to Court, with the hope of obtaining the reward of their services. Consequently, as very few men were left with him, the *zamíndárs*, who had long nourished revenge against him in their hearts, and were always lying in wait for him, took advantage of the opportunity, and having assembled from all sides, burnt the bridge which was the only means of his receiving succour, and engaged openly in rebellion.   su-lla Khán, having taken refuge in the fort, maintained his position for two or three days with great difficulty. As there were no provisions in the fort, and the enemy had cut off the supply of water, he resolved to die with the few men he had with him, and he gave proofs of the most

---

[1] The text says the contrary.

[2] It takes a slight turn to the north before joining the Kishenganga; but after the junction, they flow together towards the south.

* [End of Sir H. M. Elliot's translation.]

determined courage. Many of his men were slain, and many captured. When this news reached my ears, I appointed Jalál, son of Diláwar Khán, in whose forehead shone the marks of intelligence and worth, and who had shown much enterprise in the conquest of Kishtiwár, to extirpate the wretched rebels; and having conferred on him the rank of 1000 and the command of 600 horse, ordered the retainers of his father, who were now enlisted among the special servants of the throne, together with part of the Kashmír army, a large body of *zamindárs*, and some matchlockmen, to reinforce him. Rájá Sang Ram, the *zamindár* of Jammú, was also ordered to attack with his force from the Jammú hills, and it was now hoped that the rebels would soon be punished.

Conquest of Kángrá.

[On Monday, 5th Muharram, the joyful intelligence of the conquest of the fort of Kángrá arrived. * * Kángrá is an ancient fort, situated in the hills north of Lahore, and has been renowned for its strength and security from the days of its foundation. The *zamindárs* of the Panjáb believe that this fort has never passed into the possession of another tribe, and that no stranger's hand has ever prevailed against it; but God knows! Since the day that the sword of Islám and the glory of the Muhammadan religion have reigned in Hindústán, not one of the mighty Sultáns had been able to reduce this fort. Sultán Fíroz Sháh, a monarch of great power, besieged it for a long time; but he found that the place was so strong and secure, that it was impossible to reduce it so long as the garrison had provisions. * ' When this humble individual ascended the throne, the capture of this fort was the first of all his designs. He sent Murtazá Khán, governor of the Panjáb, against it with a large force, but Murtazá died before its reduction was accomplished. Chaupar Mal, son of Rájá Bású, was afterwards sent against it; but that traitor rebelled, his army was broken up, and the fall of the fortress was deferred. Not long after, the traitor was made prisoner, and was executed and went to hell, as has been recorded in the proper place. Prince Khurram was afterwards sent against it with a strong force, and many nobles were directed to support him. In the month of Shawwál, 1029 H., his forces invested the place, the trenches were portioned out, and the ingress of provisions was completely stopped. In time the fortress was in difficulty, no corn or food remained in the place, but for four months longer the men lived upon dry fodder, and similar things which they boiled and ate ; but when death stared them in the face, and no hope of deliverance remained, the place surrendered on Monday, Muharram 1, 1031.]

Saffron.[1]

As the saffron was in blossom, His Majesty left the city to go to Pámpúr,[2] which is the only place in Kashmír where it flourishes. Every parterre, every field, was, as far as the eye could reach, covered with flowers. The stem inclines towards the ground. The flower has five petals of a violet colour, and three stigmas producing saffron are found within it, and that is the purest saffron. In an ordinary year, 400 *maunds*, or 3200 Khurásání *maunds*, are produced. Half belongs to the Government, half to the cultivators, and a *sír* sells for ten rupees ;[3] but the price sometimes varies a little. It is the established custom to weigh the flowers, and give them to the manufacturers, who take them home and extract the saffron from them, and upon giving the extract, which amounts to about one-fourth weight of the flower, to the public officers, they receive in return an equal weight of salt, in lieu of money wages ; for salt is not produced in Kashmír, and even in the beauty of the inhabitants there

[1] [See *suprá*, p. 304.]

[2] This place still maintains its reputation. Von Hügel tells us, that saffron is produced almost exclusively in the district of Pámpúr, on the right bank of the Jhelam, from three distinct varieties of crocus ; the root of one sort continues productive for fifteen years ; of another, for eight ; of the third, for five.—*Kaschmir*, vol. ii. 275.

[3] Mr. Pereira states that one grain of good saffron contains the stigmata and styles of nine flowers ; hence 4320 flowers are required to yield one ounce of saffron.

is but very little, *i.e.* they have but little expression.[1] They
import salt from Hindústán. * * *

The next day the fortunate camp was pitched at Rájaur. The
people of Rájaur were originally Hindús. Sultán Fíroz converted them. Nevertheless, their chiefs are still styled Rájás.
Practices which prevailed during the times of their ignorance
are still observed amongst them. Thus, wives immolate themselves alive on the funeral pyres of their husbands, and bury
themselves alive in their graves. It was reported that, only a
few days ago, a girl of twelve years old had buried herself with
her husband. Indigent parents strangle their female offspring
immediately after birth. They associate and intermarry with
Hindús—giving and taking daughters. As for taking, it does
not so much matter; but, as for giving their own daughters—
heaven protect us! Orders were issued prohibiting these practices for the future, and punishments enjoined for their infraction.

Sháh Jahán sent to the Dakhin.

[In these happy days, when I was enjoying myself in hunting
and travelling in Kashmír, successive despatches arrived from
the Dakhin. When the royal Court left the capital, evil-disposed
men in the Dakhin, failing in duty and loyalty, raised the
standard of rebellion. They got many of the dependencies of
Ahmadnagar and Birár into their power, and the despatches
related how they were maintaining themselves by plunder and
devastation, and were burning and destroying ships and pro-
vender. On the former occasion, when I marched with the
Imperial army to effect the conquest of the Dakhin, Khurram,
who commanded the advance, arrived at Burhánpúr. The insurgents, with that craft which distinguishes them, made him
their intercessor, and abandoned the Imperial territory. They
presented large offerings of money and valuables as tribute, and

---

[1] *Malábat* is the word, and a double meaning is intended. *Malábat* not only
means saltness as well as expression, but a dark complexion in opposition to *Labábat*,
"fairness." These meanings are not in the dictionaries, though there is some approach to them in Freytag. Nevertheless, they are of common application.

engaged to remain quiet and loyal. At the instance of Khurram, I remained for some days in the palace of Shádíábád at Mái.dú, and consented to forgive their misdeeds. Now that they had once more thrown off their allegiance, it was my wish to send the Imperial army again under the command of Khurram, to inflict upon them the punishment they deserved, and to make them an example and warning for others. But he was engaged in the siege of Kángrá, and many experienced officers were with him on that service, so that for some days I could not determine what to do.

Letters arrived one after the other, reporting that the insurgents having gathered strength, numbered nearly 60,000 horse, and had occupied many parts of the Imperial dominions. The forces which had been left in occupation had taken the field, and for three months had been operating against the rebels, over whom they had obtained several advantages. But the rebels employed themselves in plundering and laying waste the country about the Imperial forces, and there was no road left open for the supply of provisions, so great want arose. Suddenly they descended from the Bálághát, and stopped at Bálápúr. Emboldened by their impunity, they meditated a raid round Bálápúr. The Imperial forces numbered 6000 or 7000 horse, and in some fighting which occurred, they lost their baggage. Many were killed or taken, and the rebels returned unmolested and plundering to their quarters. Gathering forces from all sides, the rebels advanced fighting as far as Azdú. Nearly 1000 men fell on both sides. They stayed at Bálápúr three months. The scarcity in the royal camp became very great, and many of the men fled and joined the rebels. The royal force retreated to Burhánpúr, and was followed and besieged there by the rebels. They remained for six months round Burhánpúr, and took possession of several districts in Birár and Khándesh, where they by force exacted contributions from the people. The royal forces suffered great hardships and privations, and being unable to endure longer, they came out of the city (?). This increased the insolence and pride of the rebels. By the favour of God, Kángrá had fallen, and so on Friday, the 4th De, I sent Khurram to the Dakhin, and I conferred upon him ten *krors* of *dams*, to be collected from the country after its conquest. * * I now turned back on my return to the capital.]

Sixteenth Year of the Reign.

[The Nau-roz of my sixteenth year fell on the 27th Rabí'u-s sání, 1030 H. (10th March, 1621 A.D.).]

Fall of a Meteoric Stone.

One of the most surprising events of the time is the following : On the morning of the 30th Farwardín of the present year, a very loud and dreadful noise arose from the east, in one of the villages of the *pargana* of Jálandhar, and almost frightened the inhabitants to death. In the midst of the noise a light fell on the earth from the sky, and the people thought that fire was going to fall. After a moment, when the noise had subsided, and the people, who were much confounded and alarmed, had come to their senses, they sent a runner to Muhammad Sa'íd, the *'A'mil* of the *pargana*, and informed him of the phenomenon. The *'A'mil* immediately rode to the village, and saw the place with his own eyes. The land for about ten or twelve yards in length and breadth was so burnt that not a blade of grass or herbage was found there. The ground was yet warm. He ordered it to be dug, and the deeper it was dug the warmer it was found. At last a piece of iron appeared, which was as hot as if it had been just taken out of a furnace. After some time it became cool. He took it to his residence, and having put it into a bag and sealed it up, he sent it to me. It was weighed in my presence, and found to weigh 160 *tolas*. I ordered Ustád Dáúd to make a sword, a dagger, and a knife from it, and to bring them to me; but he represented that it would not bear hammering, but would break into pieces. I ordered that if that was the case it should be mixed with other iron. Accordingly three parts of the meteoric iron were mixed with one part of common iron, and two swords, one knife, and one dagger, were made and presented to me. The watering was made on them with the other kind of iron. The sword bent like the genuine *Almási* swords or those of the Dakhin, and again became perfectly straight. I ordered them to be tried before me, and they cut exceedingly well, equal to the best tempered swords.

War in the Dakhin.

[On the 4th Khurdád, letters arrived from Khurram. When the Imperial forces reached Újjain, a letter arrived from the force which held Mándú, with the information that a rebel force had boldly crossed the Nerbadda, had burnt several villages in sight of the fort, and was engaged in plundering. The commander-in-chief sent forward Khwája Abú-l Hasan, at the head of 5000 horse, to march rapidly and inflict punishment on the rebels. The Khwája arrived at daybreak on the banks of the Nerbadda, but they had got information of his approach, and had crossed over just before he came. The royal forces pursued them for nearly four *kos*, and put many of them to the sword. The rebels retreated to Burhánpúr. Khurram then wrote to the Khwája, directing him to remain on that side of the river until he himself arrived. Shortly afterwards Khurram joined the advanced force, and they marched rapidly to Burhánpúr. On their approach the rebels took to flight, and removed to a distance from Burhánpúr. For two years the royal forces had been shut up in Burhánpúr, and had suffered greatly from want of food and supplies. They were greatly in want of horses. The army remained there nine days to refit, and during that time thirty *lacs* of rupees and many coats were distributed among the Imperial soldiers. They had no sooner begun to move, than the rebels, unable to make any resistance, fled. The royal forces pursued, and put many of them to the sword. Thus giving them no time for repose, they drove them to Khirki, which was the abode of Nizámu-l Mulk and other rebels. But before the royal army arrived, the rebels carried off Nizámu-l Mulk with all his family and dependents to the fortress of Daulatábád. Some of their men were scattered about the country.

The royal forces stayed three days at Khirki, and so destroyed that town, which had taken twenty years to build, that it will hardly recover its splendour for the next twenty years. Having destroyed this place, it was determined to march to Ahmadnagar, which was besieged by a rebel force, and after driving off the besiegers, and revictualling and reinforcing the place, to return. With this determination they marched to Pattan. The rebel now resorted to artifice, and sent envoys and nobles to express his repentance and ask forgiveness. He promised ever afterwards to remain loyal, and not to depart from the old arrangement, and also to send his tribute and a sum as an indemnity to the Imperial Court. It happened that just at this time there was a great want of provisions in the royal camp, and the news arrived that the rebels, who were laying siege to Ahmadnagar, being frightened at the approach of the royal army, had moved off to a distance. So a reinforcement and some cash to supply his needs were sent to Khanjar Khán (the commandant). Having made every necessary provision, the royal army set out on its return. After much entreaty on the part of the rebel, it was settled that, besides the territory which was formerly held by the Imperial officers, a space of fourteen *kos* beyond should be relinquished, and a sum of fifty *lacs* of rupees should be sent to the Imperial treasury.]

Illness of Jahángír.

[I have before mentioned that on the day of the *Dasahra*, when I was in Kashmír, I was seized with a catching and shortness of breath. This was charged entirely to the moisture of the atmosphere. In the air-passages on my left side near the heart, an oppression and catching was felt. It gradually increased and became fixed. * * A course of warm medicine gave me a little relief; but when I crossed the mountains, the violence of the malady increased. On the present occasion I took goat's milk for several days, and I bethought me of the camel's milk (I had formerl. taken), but neither of them did me any good. [*Treatment by various doctors.*] In despair of obtaining any relief from medicine, I gave up all doctoring, and threw myself upon the mercy of the Universal Physician. As I found relief in drinking, contrary to my habit, I resorted to it in the daytime, and by degrees I carried it to excess. When the weather became hot, the evil effects of this became apparent, and my weakness and suffering increased. Núr Jahán Begam, whose sense and experience exceeded that of the physicians, in her kindness and devotion, exerted herself to reduce the quantity of my potations, and to provide me with suitable and soothing preparations. Although I had before discarded the doctors and their advice, I now had faith in her attention. She gradually reduced the quantity of wine I took, and guarded me against unsuitable food and improper things. My hope is, that the True Physician will give me a perfect cure. * *

When intelligence of my illness reached my son Parwez, he did not wait for a summons, but set off instantly to see me, and on the 14th of the month, that kind and dutiful son came into my presence. I seated him on the throne near me, and although I adjured him and forbad him, he burst into tears, and showed the deepest concern. I took his hand, drew him to my side, and pressed him affectionately to my bosom. I showed him every attention and kindness, and I hope that his life and prosperity may be prolonged.

Journey to Kángrá.

The extreme heat of Ágra was uncongenial to my constitution, so on the 12th Ábán, in the sixteenth year of my reign, I started for the mountain country on the north, intending, if the climate proved suitable, to build a town somewhere on the banks of the Ganges, to which I might resort in the hot weather. If I could not find a place that suited me, I intended to proceed further towards Kashmír. * * On the 7th De. I arrived at Hardwár on the Ganges, and there halted; but as the climate of the skirts of the mountains was not pleasant, and I found no place appropriate for a residence, I resolved to proceed farther to the mountains of Jammú and Kángrá. * * On the 14th, I arrived at the village of Bahlún, a dependency of Sibá, and as I had a great desire for the air of Kángrá, I left my great camp at this place, and proceeded onwards with a few special attendants and servants towards the fortress.

I'timádu-d daula was ill, so I left him behind with the camp under the charge of Sádik Khán *Mir-bakhshi*. On the following day the intelligence was brought that a change for the worse had come over the Khán, and the signs of dissolution were manifest. Moved by the distress of Núr Jahán Begam, and by the affection I had for him, I could proceed no further, so I returned to the camp. At the close of the day I went to see him. He was at times insensible, and Núr Jahán, who was by my side, made signs and asked if I perceived (his critical state). I stayed by his pillow two hours. Whenever he came to his senses, his words were intelligible and sensible. On the 17th of the month he died, and I felt inexpressible sorrow at the loss of such an able and faithful minister, and so wise and kind a friend.

After this I went on towards Kángrá, and after four days' march encamped on the river Bán-gangá. * * On the 24th of the month I went to pay a visit to the fortress, and I gave orders that the *kázi*, the Chief Justice, and others learned in the law of Islám, should accompany me, and perform the ceremonies required by our religion. After passing over about half a *kos*, we mounted to the fort, and then by the grace of God prayers were said, the *khutba* was read, a cow was killed, and other things were done, such as had never been done before from the foundation of the fort to the present time. All this was done in my presence, and I bowed myself in thanks to the Almighty for this great conquest which no previous monarch had been able to accomplish. I ordered a large mosque to be built in the fortress. * *

A letter from Khurram informed me that Khusrú had died of colic.]

SEVENTEENTH YEAR OF THE REIGN.

[The Nau-roz of the seventeenth year of my reign fell on — Jumáda-l awwal, 1031 (March, 1622).

A despatch arrived from the son of Khán Jahán, reporting that Sháh 'Abbás, King of Persia, had laid siege to the fort of Kandahár with the forces of 'Irák and Khurásán. I gave orders for calling troops from Kashmír, and Khwája Abú-l Hasan *Díwán* and Sádik Khán *Bakhshí* were sent on in advance of me to Lahore, to organize the forces as the princes brought them up from the Dakhin. Gujarát, Bengal, and Bihár, and as the nobles came from their *jágírs* and assembled, and then to send them on in succession to the son of Khán Jahán at Multán. Artillery, mortars, elephants, treasure, arms, and equipments were also to be sent on thither . . . For such an army 100,000 bullocks or more would be needed. * *.

Zainu-l 'Ábidín, whom I had sent to summon Khurram, returned and reported that the Prince would come after he had passed the rainy season in the fort of Mándú. When I read and understood the contents of the Prince's letter, I was not at all pleased, or rather I was displeased. I consequently wrote a *farmán* to the effect, that as it was his intention to wait till after the rains, he was to send me the great *amírs* and officers I had placed under his command, especially the Saiyids of Bárha and Bokhárá, the Shaikhzádas, the Afgháns, and Rájpúts.]

Rebellion of Sháh Jahán.

[Intelligence was brought that Khurram had seized upon some of the *jágírs* of Núr Jahán Begam and Prince Shahriyár. He had fought with Ashrafu-l Mulk, an officer of Shahriyár's, who had been appointed *faujdár* of Dholpúr and the country round, and several men had been killed on both sides. I had been offended by his delaying at the fort of Mándú, and by his improper and foolish statements in his letters, and I had perceived by his insolence that his mind was estranged. Upon hearing of this further intelligence, I saw that, notwithstanding all the favour and kindness I had shown him, his mind was perverted. I accordingly sent Rájá Roz-afzún, one of my oldest servants, to inquire into the reasons of this boldness and presumption. I also sent him a *farmán*, directing him to attend to his own affairs, and not to depart from the strict line of duty. He was to be content with the *jágírs* that had been bestowed upon him from the Imperial Exchequer. I warned him not to come to me, but to send all the troops which had been required from him for the campaign against Kandahár. If he acted contrary to my commands, he would afterwards have to repent. * * * When Khurram's son was ill, I made a vow that, if God would spare his life, I would never shoot an animal again with my own hand. For all my love of shooting, I kept my vow for five years to the present time; but now that I was offended with Khurram, I resolved to go out shooting again.

On the 24th I crossed the Jhelam. On the same day Afzal Khán, *díwán* of Khurram, arrived with a letter, in which Khurram endeavoured to make excuses for his undutiful actions. He hoped also that by Afzal Khán's persuasion and plausibility he might obtain forgiveness; but I took no notice of him, and showed him no favour.

Letters arrived from I'tibár Khán and other of my officers whom I had left at A'gra, stating that Khurram persisted in his perverse course, and preferring the way of disobedience to the path of duty, had taken a decided step in the road to perdition by marching upon A'gra. For this reason, said I'tibár, I have not deemed it advisable to send on the treasure, but have busied myself in making preparation for a siege. A letter from A'saf Khán also arrived, stating that this ungrateful son had torn away the veil of decency, and had broken into open rebellion;

that he (the Khán) had received no certain intelligence of his movements, so, not considering it expedient to move the treasure, he had set out alone to join me.

On receiving this intelligence, I crossed the river at Sultánpúr, and marched to inflict punishment on this ill-starred son (siyáh-bakht). I issued an order that from this time forth he should be called "Wretch" (be-daulat).[1]

On the 1st Isfandármuz, I received a letter from I'tibár Khán, informing me that the rebel had advanced with all speed to the neighbourhood of Ágra, my capital, in the hope of getting possession of it before it could be put in a state of preparation. On reaching Fathpúr, he found that his hope was vain, so he remained there. He was accompanied by Khán-khánán (Mirzá Khán) and his son; and by many other amírs who held office in the Dakhin and in Gujarát, and had now entered upon the path of rebellion and perfidy. * * The rebels took nine lacs of rupees from the house of Lashkar Khán, and everywhere they seized upon whatever they found serviceable in the possession of my adherents. Khán-khánán, who had held the exalted dignity of being my tutor, had now turned rebel, and in the seventieth year of his age had blackened his face with ingratitude. But he was by nature a rebel and traitor. His father, at the close of his days, had acted in the same shameful way towards my revered father. He had but followed the course of his father, and disgraced himself in his old age—

> "The wolf's whelp will grow a wolf,
> E'en though reared with man himself."

After I had passed through Sirhind, troops came flocking in from all directions, and by the time I reached Dehlí, such an army had assembled, that the whole country was covered with men as far as the eye could reach. Upon being informed that the rebel had advanced from Fathpúr, I marched to Dehlí.

In this war I appointed Mahábat Khán commander-in-chief

---

[1] [Here follows the passage quoted in page 281 supra.]

of the army, and 'Abdu lla Khán to the command of the
advanced force of chosen and experienced troops. His business
was to go on a *kos* in advance, to collect information, and take
possession of the roads. I forgot that he was an old companion
of the rebel; but the result was that he communicated information about my army to the rebel.]

EIGHTEENTH YEAR OF THE REIGN.

[The eighteenth year of my reign commenced on 20th Jumáda-l
awwal, 1032 H. (10th March, 1623). On this day intelligence
was brought that the rebel had advanced near to Mathurá, and
had encamped in the *pargana* of Sháhpúr. * * The next intelligence was that he had deviated from the direct course, and had
gone twenty *kos* to the left. Sundar Ráí, who was the leader in
this rebellion, Dáráb son of Khán-khánán, and many other *amírs*,
had been sent on with the army against me. The command was
nominally held by Dáráb, but Sundar was the real commander,
and the prop of the revolt. They encamped near Bilúchpúr. I
sent forward 25,000 horse under A'saf Khán, and he was opposed
by Kásim Khán and others. * * The Almighty has at all times
and in all places been gracious unto me; so when 'Abdu-lla
Khán went over to the enemy with 10,000 men under his command, and a great disaster menaced my army, a bullet directed
by fate killed Sundar, and his fall made the rebels waver.
Khwája Abú-l Hasan drove back the force opposed to him, A'saf
Khán also brought up his division opportunely, and we achieved
a great victory. * * .

When the rebel passed near Amber,[1] the birth-place and abode of
Rájá Mán Singh, he sent a party of men to plunder it, and lay it
waste. * * I also learnt that he had sent Jagat Singh, son of Rájá
Bású, to stir up disturbances in his native land in the Panjáb. * *

On the 25th Urdíbihisht, I appointed my son Sháh Parwez
to the command of the army operating against the rebel. He
was to have the supreme command, but Mu'tamadu-d daula al

---

[1] [In the province of Ajmír.]

Káhira Mahábat Khán was charged with the general direction
of the army. Khán-i 'álam, Mahárájá Gaj Singh, Fázil Khán,
Rashíd Khán, Rájá Giridhar, Rájá Rám Dás, and others were
also sent with him. The force consisted of 40,000 horse, with
suitable artillery, and twenty *lacs* of rupees were assigned to it. * *
On the 30th, agreeing with 19th Rajab, 1034, I encamped by the
tank of Áná-ságar, within sight of Ajmír.

When the Prince's army passed over the mountains of
Chándá, and entered Málwá, Sháh Jahán came out of the fort
of Mándú with 20,000 horse, 600 elephants, and powerful
artillery, with the intention of giving battle. * * Mahábat Khán
opened communications with several persons, who, through apprehension or compulsion, had joined the army of the rebel, and
they, perceiving that his case was hopeless, wrote to Mahábat,
asking for assurances of safety. Sháh Jahán, not daring to
risk a general action, and thinking always of his retreat, sent
his elephants over the Nerbadda. He then sent his forces against
the royal army near the village of Káliya; but he himself, with
Khán-khánán and several others, remained a *kos* in the rear.
Barkandáz Khán, who had been in correspondence with Mahábat,
and had received his promise, when the opposing armies approached each other, seized the opportunity of coming over to
the royal army with the body of matchlockmen that he commanded. Rustam also, one of the chief and most trusted
officers of the rebel, received assurances from Mahábat, and came
over with several other officers. When Sháh Jahán heard of
this, he gave up resistance, and, being unable to place reliance
upon any one, he determined to fly. With his forces in disorder,
he crossed the Nerbadda, and several of his followers took
advantage of the confusion to join the royal army.

Sháh Jahán, having crossed the Nerbadda, kept all the boats
on his side, and placed strong guards over the fords. Leaving
Bairam Beg *Bakhshi* with a force of his most trusty soldiers and
men of the Dakhin, and with the artillery drawn up by the
river, he himself went off towards the fort of Asír and Burhán-

púr. At this time his men caught a messenger whom Khán-khánán had sent to Mahábat Khán. He sent for the Kháu, and showed him the letter taken from the messenger.. Khán-khánán endeavoured to excuse himself, but could not give a satisfactory answer. An order was accordingly given that he and Dáráb and his other sons should be kept under arrest.

Rustam Khán, Muhammad. Murád, and several others who had abandoned the service of the rebel, and had paid their respects to my dutiful son, according to orders weie sent to my Court, and were received by me. Rustam Khán received a *mansab* of 5000, and 4000 horse. Muhammad Murád a *mansab* of 1000, and 500 horse, and prospects of future promotion were held out to them.

When the rebel Sháh Jahán reached Asír, he placed Khán-khánan, Dáráb, and all his other children in confinement in the upper part of the fortress. He remained there three or four days, attending to the victualling and preparation of the fortress, which he placed under the command of Gopál Dás, a Rájpút. * * When he departed, he left some of his women and superfluous things there in charge of Gopál; but he took with him his three wives, his children, and such maids as were necessary. His first intention was to leave Khán-khánán and his children prisoners there; but he changed his mind, and carried them with him to Burhánpúr. * * Mahábat Khán was very desirous to separate Khán-khánán from the rebel, and thus to promote a peace. Sháh Jahán also, in the strait he then was, took Khán-khánán out of confinement, and bound him by oath upon the Kurán to be faithful. To give force to the oath and agreement, he took him into his female apartments, and giving him the privileges of a near relation, presented to him his wives and children, and, with tears and great earnestness, said, " In case of evil falling upon me, I trust myself and the honour of my family to you ; something must be done, that I may proceed no further in this wretched and miserable course."

Khán-khánán separated from him, intent upon peace, and proceeded towards the imperial army. It was arranged that he should stay on that side of the river to carry on the negociations for peace. But before he reached the bank of the river, some dashing young men of the royal army one night found a place which the rebels had left unguarded, and passed over the river. This caused some dismay, but Bairam Beg gallantly resolved to contest the passage. While he was getting his forces together some more men passed over, and the same night the rebels retreated. Khán-khánán was left in a difficult position, he did not know whether to advance or retreat. But the men of my son's army continually pressed forward, and Khán-khánán was relieved from the trammels of rebellion, and was presented by Mahábat Khán to my son.

Sháh Jahán, when he heard of the defection of Khán-khánán, the passage of the river by the Imperial troops, and the retreat of Bairam Beg, fell back. Notwithstanding heavy rain and inundations, he crossed the river Matí in a wretched state, and went off towards the Dakhin. In the confusion many officers, who willingly or unwillingly had joined him, now separated from him.

On the 9th Ábán, Khawás Khán brought a despatch from Prince Parwez and Mahábat Khán, informing me that they had reached Burhánpúr, but that many men had fallen in the rear in consequence of the violence of the rain. But acting in obedience to orders, they had taken no rest, and had pressed on in pursuit of the rebel across the river (Táptí). The fugitives, on hearing of their arrival, continued their flight in disorder, and lost many of their animals through the heavy rain, and the mud and mire. The royal forces then continued the pursuit to the *pargana* of Ankot. Forty *kos* from Burhánpúr. * * The rebel then went on to the territories of Kutbu-l Mulk. When my son Parwez found that the rebel had quitted my dominions, he and Mahábat and all the others returned to Burhánpúr on the 1st Ábán.

It was arrived that Sháh Jahán, with Dáráb and other of the territory of Kutbu-l Mulk, and

was making for Orissa and Bengal. On the way they had to
endure great hardships, and many of the rebel's companions
abandoned him when they found opportunity. * * After performing a long march, Sháh Jahán arrived at Machhlí (Masuli-
patam), which belonged to Kutbu-l Mulk. When his arrival
there became known, Kutbu-l Mulk sent one of his people to
the fugitive, and gave him every kind of relief and assistance in
money and provisions. He also directed his margrave to convoy
the fugitive safely out of his dominions, and he further appointed
grain-dealers and *zamindárs* to attend his camp, and supply it
with corn and other necessaries. * *]

NINETEENTH YEAR OF THE REIGN.

[The *Nau-roz* of my nineteenth year corresponded with 29th
Jamáda-l awwal, 1033 (10th March, 1624).

Intelligence next came that the rebel had reached the confines
of Orissa. Upon which I issued a *farmán* to Prince Parwez,
Mahábat Khan, and the other nobles who had been sent to
support them, with orders to provide, as far as possible, for the
safety of that province, and to march towards Allahábád and
Bihár. * * Upon the arrival of these orders, the Prince prepared to obey, and to march towards Allahabad, notwithstanding
the violence of the rains. On the 6th Farwardin, he marched
with the Imperial army from Burhanpur to Lál Bagh; but
Mahabat Khan remained at Burhanpur, awaiting the arrival of
Mulla Muhammad Lari.

A despatch arrived from Ibrahim Beg Khan, with the information that Shah Jahan had entered the province of Orissa. The
explanation of this was, that between Orissa and the Dakhin
there is a difficult pass, on one side of which are mountains, on
the other a marsh [1] (?) and a river. In this place the ruler of
Golkonda had built a fort, and had armed it with guns and
muskets. It was impossible to pass this place without the con-

---

[1] جلبه

eent of Kutbu-l Mulk; but the escort which he had sent to conduct Sháh Jahán had enabled the rebel to pass this fortress and to enter Orissa. * * On hearing of the rebel's approach, Sálih, brother of the late Ásaf Khán, who held the *jágir* of Bardwán, put the fort in a state of defence. * * Ibráhím Khán being frightened, took refuge in Akbar-nagar,[1] where he occupied himself in gathering forces and preparing for resistance.]

[1] [Rájmahál.—Stewart's *Bengal*, p. 186.]

TATIMMA-I WÁKI'ÁT-I JAHÁNGÍRÍ

OF

MUHAMMAD HÁDÍ.

THIS work is the completion of the Memoirs noticed in the preceding article. The author is Muhammad Hádí, of whom mention has already been made. In his Preface, however, he omits the title of Kámwar Khán, which he gives himself in his other works. He tells us that he wrote when he was more than sixty years old, after transcribing the Memoirs of eighteen years with his own hand; that after having completed this task, it occurred to him that the "thirsty wanderers in the desert of history" would be dissatisfied, like himself, at reaching to the end of the eighteenth year and finding the work incomplete; and that, as he from his earliest youth had been much devoted to historical studies, he determined to complete the work to the close of Jahángír's reign, and to add an Introduction to the Memoirs, detailing the principal events of Jahángír's life previous to his accession to the throne, availing himself for this purpose of several trustworthy manuscripts. He has done this satisfactorily, but without adding anything to our previous knowledge; for he copies his authorities almost verbatim, and especially the *Ikbál-náma*, from which he has borrowed most largely. At the end of the Introduction, he tells us that he hoped some day to be able to write a brief history of the entire reign of Sháh Jahán from beginning to end, and to append it to the history of Jahángír. He may be considered to have accomplished this task in the *Tárikh-i Chaghatái.*

The copies I have seen of this work are annexed to manuscripts of the authentic Memoirs, and perhaps the continuation is not to be found separate. [It is so annexed to the Memoirs in the MS. belonging to the Royal Asiatic Society.]

[The work, being a completion of the Memoirs, and appended to them, is taken out of its chronological order. Its exact date is not known, but the author's other work, the *Táríkh-i Chaghatái*, comes down to 1137 A.H. (A.D. 1724).

The Introduction is a brief narrative of the important events in the life of Jahángír prior to his accession, and is borrowed from Mirzá Kámgár and other sources.

The body of the work is almost entirely a reproduction of the *Ikbál-náma;* but the Editor has translated a few passages which the author appears to have derived from another authority. The last Extract is taken from the short chapter at the end on the ministers of Jahángír; the translation of this is by an unknown contributor, but it has been greatly altered by Sir H. M. Elliot.]

The Introduction comprises 28 pages, and the continuation of the Memoirs 88 pages of 17 lines each.

EXTRACTS.

NINETEENTH YEAR OF THE REIGN.

[The New Year began on a day corresponding with 29th Jumáda-l awwal, 1033 H. (10th March, 1624 A.D.).

When Sultán Parwez and Mahábat Khán arrived near Alláh-ábád, 'Abdu-lla Khán raised the siege and returned to Jhaunsí. Daryá Khán held the bank of the river in force, and had carried all the boats over to his own side; the passage of the Imperial army was thus delayed for some days. The Prince and Mahábat Khán encamped on the other side of the river. Daryá Khán held the fords, but the *zamíndárs* of the neighbourhood showed their loyalty, and collected thirty boats[1] from various parts, and guided the royal forces over at a spot some *kos* higher up. Daryá Khán held his position to contest the passage until he heard

---

[1] [The phrase here used for boats is *manzil-i kishti*, which seems to be of the same character as *zanjír-i-fíl* and *katár-i shutar*. See a note of Sir H. Elliot's in Vol. V. p. 108, where the word *sarái* is used in connexion with ships.]

that the royal army had crossed. He then knew that it was no longer tenable, and fell back to Jaunpúr. 'Abdu-lla Khán and Rájá Bhím proceeded to Jaunpúr, and counselled a movement to Benares; so Shál Jahán sent his female and attendants to Rohtás, and himself proceeded to Benares. He was joined by 'Abdu-lla Khán, Rájá Bhím, and Daryá Khán, and having arrived at Benares, passed over the Ganges, and halted on the river Túnus. Prince Parwez and Mahábat Khán, having arrived at Damdama,[1] they left A'ká Muhammad Zamán Tehéráni there, while they passed over the Ganges with the intention of crossing over the Túnus. Sháh Jahán, leaving Khán-daurán in charge of his position, crossed the Ganges, and confronted Muhammad Zamán, who fell back to Jhaunsí. Khán-daurán advanced in full confidence, and Muhammad Zamán hastened to meet him. A sharp action followed. Khán-daurán was defeated, and his soldiers abandoned him. Being left alone, he struggled and fought desperately in every direction until he was killed. His head was sent to Prince Parwez. Rustam Khán, an old servant of Sháh Jahán's, now left him and joined Prince Parwez. He said it was a good thing that the traitor[2] (Khán-daurán) had been killed. Jahángír Kulí, son of Khán-i 'azam, who was present, said, " No one can call him rebel or traitor, a more devoted man cannot exist, for he served his master to the death, and what more could he do ! Even now his head is raised above all."

Sháh Jahán took his departure from Bengal, and proceeded towards the Dakhin. Mukhlis Khán then went on the wings of haste to Prince Parwez, to send him and his *amírs* on to the Dakhin. * * A despatch arrived from Asad Khán, the *Bakhshí* of the Dakhin, written at Burhánpúr, to the effect that Ya'kúb Khán Habshí, with 10,000 horse, had arrived at Malkápúr, ten *kos* from the city, and that Sarbuland Rái had gone out of the city with the intention of attacking him. Upon this, strict injunc-

---

[1] [*damdama* means " a battery," but here it would rather appear to be a proper name.]

[2] [*haram-khur.*]

tions were sent forbidding him to fight until reinforcements arrived.

At the beginning of 1034 A.H. Sháh Jahán arrived in the Dakhin. Malik 'Ambar tendered him assistance, and sent a force under the command of Ya'kúb Khán Habshí to Burhánpúr to plunder. He communicated this movement to Sháh Jahán, who proceeded in that direction, and pitched his camp at Dewalgánw. The Prince then sent 'Abdu-lla Khán to join Ya'kúb Khán, and lay siege to Burhánpúr. He himself followed, and pitched his tent in the Lál Bágh, in the outskirts of the city. Rao Ratan, and other Imperial officers who were in the place, did their best to put it in a state of defence, and took every precaution to secure it. Sháh Jahán ordered 'Abdu-lla to assail the town on one side, and Sháh Kulí Khán on the other. The besieged, by dint of numbers and by hard fighting, held 'Abdu-lla in check; but Sháh Kulí's division breached the walls, and made their way inside.

Sarbuland Ráí then left a force to keep 'Abdu-lla Khán in check, and hastened to attack Sháh Kulí. Several of Sháh Kulí Khán's men were scattered in the streets and bázárs, but he, with the few around him, stood fast in the esplanade in front of the citadel. Several of them fell. He then entered the citadel, and closed the gates. Sarbuland Ráí surrounded it, and Sháh Kulí, being hard pressed, capitulated.

Sháh Jahán then ordered a second attack to be made; but although great gallantry was exhibited, the assault failed, and several officers of distinction fell. He mounted his horse, and ordered a third assault. Great courage was again displayed, and many officers and men fell, but without success. Saiyid Ja'far received a slight wound in the neck from a bullet, but he was so frightened that he went away. His departure affected all the Dakhinís, who broke up and went away, followed by many men who were disheartened by failure.

Intelligence now arrived, that Prince Parwez and Mahábat Khán, with the Imperial army, had reached the Nerbadda on their return, so Sháh Jahán retired to the Bálághát. 'Abdu-lla Khán separated from him, and occupied the village (*mauza'*) of Indore. * *]

TWENTIETH YEAR OF THE REIGN.

[When the raising of the siege of Burhánpúr was reported to the Emperor, he bestowed great favours on Sarbuland Rái. He gave him a *mansab* of 5000 and the title of Rám Ráj, than which there is no higher title in the Dakhin. When the siege was raised, Sháh Jahán bent his course to the Dakhin, but he was seized with illness on the way. The error of his conduct now became apparent to him, and he felt that he must beg forgiveness of his father for his offences. So with this proper feeling he wrote a letter to his father, expressing his sorrow and repentance, and begging pardon for all faults past and present. His Majesty wrote an answer with his own hand, to the effect that if he would send his sons Dárá Shukoh and Aurangzeb to Court, and would surrender Rohtás and the fortress of Asír, which were held by his adherents, full forgiveness should be given him, and the country of the Bálághát should be conferred upon him. Upon reading this, Sháh Jahán deemed it his duty to conform to his father's wishes; so, notwithstanding the love he had for his sons, he sent them to his father, with offerings of jewels, chased arms, elephants, etc., to the value of ten *lacs* of rupees. He wrote to Muzaffar Khán, directing him to surrender Rohtás to the person appointed by the Emperor, and then to come with Sultán Murád Bakhshí. He also wrote to Hayát Khán directions for surrendering Asír to the Imperial officers. Sháh Jahán then proceeded to Násik. * *

It was now reported to the Emperor that Mahábat Khán had married his daughter to Khwája Barkhurdár, the eldest son of Nakshabandí. As this marriage had been contracted without the royal consent, the Emperor was greatly offended; so he sent for the young man, and asked him why he had, contrary to rule, married the daughter of so great a noble. He was unable to give a satisfactory answer, so he was ordered to be beaten, and sent to prison. * *

The intelligence of Mahábat Khán's daring act having reached Sháh Jahán, he was greatly incensed, and notwithstanding his bodily weakness and want of warlike munitions, he resolved to go to the assistance of his father, and inflict punishment for this presumptuous deed. On the 23rd Ramazán, 1035 A.H. (7th June, 1626 A.D.), he left Násik with 1000 horse, hoping to gather forces as he proceeded. On reaching Ajmír, Rájá Kishan Singh, son of Rájá Bhím, who accompanied him, died, and 500 horsemen of the Rájá's broke up and went away, leaving only 500 men in the suite of Sháh Jahán, and these were in great distress. Unable to carry out his original intention, he resolved to do the best he could under the circumstances, and to go to Thatta, and remain for a while in that obscure place. So he proceeded from Ajmír to Nágor, and from thence through Joudhpúr and Jesalmír.]

From the Memoirs of the Wázirs.[1]

Mirzá Ghiyás Beg was so charitably disposed, that no one ever left his door dissatisfied; but in the taking of bribes he certainly was most uncompromising and fearless. 'Alí Kulí Beg Istajlú, who was educated under the instructions of Sháh Isma'íl the Second, came and entered the service of the Emperor Akbar during the period of his stay at Lahore. He there married Mirzá Ghiyás Beg's daughter, who was born in the city of Kandahár. This individual afterwards entered the service of Jahángír, who honoured him with the title of Sher-Afgan, gave him a *jágír* in Bengal, and directed him to proceed there. The close of his life and his killing of Kutbu-d dín Khán has already been related in its proper place. After he had met with his reward, and proceeded to the desert of annihilation, by the orders of the King, the officers in Bengal sent the daughter of Mirzá Ghiyás Beg, surnamed I'timádu-d daula, to His Majesty,

---

[1] [This is borrowed with little alteration from the *Ikbál-náma*, see *post*, p. 403.]

who, in the deepest affliction at the death of Kutbu-d dín Khán,
placed her on the establishment of Rukíya Sultána, one of his
father's wives, on which she continued for a long time without
any employment. However, the days of misfortune drew to a
close, and the stars of her good fortune commenced to shine, and
to wake as from a deep sleep. The bride's chamber was prepared, the bride was decorated, and desire began to arise. Hope
was happy. A key was found for closed doors, a restorative was
found for broken hearts; and on a certain New Year's festival
she attracted the love and affection of the King. She was soon
made the favourite wife of His Majesty. In the first instance
she received the title of *Núr Mahal*, "the Light of the Palace,"
and after some days *Núr Jahán Begam*, "the Queen, the Light of
the World." All her relations were elevated to the highest offices
in the State. I'timádu-d daula became Prime Minister, and
her eldest brother, Abú-l Hasan, was appointed Master of the
Ceremonies, under the title of I'timád Khán. The King and
his relatives were deprived of all power; while the servants and
eunuchs of I'timádu-d daula became Kháns and Turkháns. The
old servant called Dila Rání, who had nursed the favourite lady
of the King, superseded Hájí Koka in the appointment of super-
intendent of the female servants of the palace, and without her
seal the Sadru-s Sadúr would not pay their stipends. Núr
Jahán managed the whole affairs of the realm, and honours of
every description were at her disposal, and nothing was wanting
to make her an absolute monarch but the reading of the *khutba*
in her name.

For some time she sat at the *jharoká*,[1] and the nobles came to
make their salutations and receive her commands. Coins were
struck in her name, and the royal seal on *farmáns* bore her
signature. In short, by degrees she became, except in name, un-
disputed Sovereign of the Empire, and the King himself became

---

[1] "Every morning the Mogul comes to a window, called the *jaruco*, which looks
into the plain or open space before the palace gate, where he shows himself to the
common people."—Sir T. Rowe. In Purchas this is called *jaruco*, in Churchill
jarruco. It is a Hindi word *jharokhá*, "a lattice."

a tool in her hands. He used to say that Núr Jahán Begam has bee . selected, and is wise enough to conduct the matters of State, and that he wanted only a bottle of wine and piece of meat to keep himself merry.

Núr Jahán won golden opinions from all people. She was liberal and just to all who begged her support. She was an asylum for all sufferers, and helpless girls were married at the expense of her private purse. She must have portioned about 500 girls in her lifetime, and thousands were grateful for her generosity.